Patriots, Pirates, Heroes & Spies

Stories from Historic Philadelphia

EDITED BY

Sandra Mackenzie Lloyd

Historic
Philadelphia
INCORPORATED

Patriots, Pirates, Heroes and Spies was previously published
by Grosset & Dunlap, 2008, ISBN 978-0-448-44911-1

First printing 2012
ISBN 978-0-9855319-0-4
LCCN 2012938024

Published by Historic Philadelphia
150 South Independence Mall, West Suite 550
Philadelphia, PA 19106
phone 215-629-5801

www.historicphiladelphia.org

A hearty *Hip Hip Huzzah!*

And many thanks to our partners and friends
who have supported *Patriots, Pirates, Heroes & Spies* and
helped in the creation of this book

Table of Contents

Introduction

Patriots, Pirates, Heroes & Spies . . . This book tells twenty amazing and true stories of real people who lived in or around Philadelphia, Pennsylvania from the 1600s up through the present. They are about people like Lydia Darragh, who risked her life to deliver important secrets to General Washington, and Peter Still, an enslaved man who bought his freedom and found his family. They are also about inventors and moms, Girl Scouts and Boy Scouts — and even a cow! — because history is something made by *all* of us, whether we are young or old, rich or poor, male or female.

All the stories in this book got their start in the *Once Upon A Nation* Storytelling program created in 2005 by Historic Philadelphia, Inc. From Memorial Day to Labor Day, Storytellers bring history to life in Philadelphia and Valley Forge. They ring their storytelling bells and invite visitors to sit on beautiful semi-circular benches placed in such locations as Independence Hall, Christ Church, and Washington's Headquarters. Then the Storyteller tells . . . a story! It could be about Lydia Darragh or Peter Still, or at the Betsy Ross House, it might be about a *vexillologist* — and you can discover what that is by reading the story in this book. By moving from bench to bench, visitors hear all kinds of stories. Some are funny, some are sad, some are dramatic — but all of the stories are *true*.

This book opens a new way for people to enjoy twenty favorite *Once Upon A Nation* stories. We hope you enjoy reading these amazing and true accounts of some remarkable people and events. You may even want to try *telling* some of these stories and become a Storyteller yourself!

Lachimo, Lenape Storyteller

FOR THOUSANDS OF YEARS, Lenape villages sat along the banks of the river Wihittuck (We-hi-tuk), the river of the Lenape. The Lenape lived in small villages, in beautiful round wooden houses covered with bark.

When European settlers crossed the Atlantic Ocean, they sailed up the Wihittuck and renamed it *Delaware.* They built houses and new towns along its banks. Most of these new settlers were farmers and the Lenape welcomed them and traded peacefully with them.

William Penn was one of these Europeans. When he founded his new province of Pennsylvania in 1681, he wanted it to be a place where all people could live together in the spirit of brotherhood. He wrote letters of friendship to the Lenape and met with them to establish good relations. The peace between the Lenape and the Pennsylvanians lasted many years.

But as the province and city grew, and more Europeans arrived, it became harder for the small Lenape villages to survive. So the Lenape began to move, often into less friendly territories. Many ended their journey in Oklahoma where the Lenape — now called the Delaware — live today.

Though far from their original home, stories survive from those ancient days,

> before the cities,
>> before the towns,
>>> before the farms and the tiny
>>> settlements along the Delaware. . . .

Along the Wihittuck . . .

Come back to that time in the valley of the Lenape. The modern city of Philadelphia vanishes into the mists of the past, replaced by great forests and small Lenape villages. During the spring planting season, everyone is at work, even the children. In the summer and fall, people tend fields, hunt, and trade goods with other villages.

But the winter is different. The Lenape stay close to home, safe in their villages. This is the season for stories. This is when Lachimo (la-chi-mo) the storyteller travels. He is always greeted warmly and welcomed into the big house under the dome where everyone waits to hear Lachimo's stories.

The first story is always the same, The Story of the Creation, the story of Kishelamàwa'kàn (ke-shal-a-mak-kan).

Kishelamàwa'kàn, the creator, made the
Spirit Beings, rock, fire, water and wind, and these
powerful spirits made the world.

Rock made the earth, fire made the sun, water
made the rains and wind made the breath of life, our
minds, our knowledge and our songs.

The story continues. It is long and goes deep into the
night.

When it is over some of the adults are ready for sleep,
but the children are restless and begin to shout for another.
It is already late. The story was long. Lachimo nods. Perhaps
one more, a short one. The children know which one they
want.

There are many storytellers and hundreds of tales, but everyone knows Mànàka'has (ma-na-ka-a-has), Rainbow Crow.
This is what the children want.

Lachimo raises his hand and there is silence, all gather
once again. Lachimo begins.

Before wind breathed life into man, the animals
were alone on the earth. When the first snows began
to fall, the animals did not know what to do. As
the snow became deeper and deeper, small animals
disappeared under it. The animals became worried
and held a council.

"One of us must travel to the home of Kishelamàwa'kàn and ask him to stop the snow."

"I will go," said Rainbow Crow, his colorful feathers shining in the falling snow.

Up he flew. Past the clouds, past the stars, until he reached the home of Kishelamàwa'kàn.

When he arrived, Rainbow Crow began to sing and his song was so beautiful that Kishelamàwa'kàn offered him a gift.

"Make the snows end," pleaded Rainbow Crow.

"This I can not," said Kishelamàwa'kàn, "but I will give you fire to keep you warm in the winter."

With that, the creator handed Rainbow Crow a burning stick and told him to hurry back to earth before it went out.

As Rainbow Crow flew back to the animals, the fire darkened his rainbow feathers until they were black and smoke got into his mouth so his beautiful singing voice became cracked . . . caw caw!

When he returned with the first fire, the snows melted and all the animals cheered for Mànàka'has.

Rainbow Crow flew away, and alone he wept. His beautiful colorful feathers were black and his song was gone.

Kishelamàwa'kàn heard Crow crying and came down to him.

The creator looked at Crow and said, "Soon

I will create man and he will take the fire, but for what you have done, I give you another gift. Crow will always be free. No one will ever capture or hunt you, and in your black feathers will shine and reflect all the colors of the world."

Crow looked and saw the tiny rainbows shining in his black feathers. He was happy again, and proud.

Lachimo ends his story and the village is silent. Slowly the Lenape rise. Young and old, strong hunters, small children, even the revered elders walk up to the well-traveled storyteller and honor him. *Wanìshi* (wa-ni-che) they each say. Thank you.

When we tell the stories of the Lenape, we honor the past. We keep the stories alive. *Wanìshi.*

The Lenape and William Penn

THE LENAPE had long lived in what became Pennsylvania and New Jersey. They were chiefly farmers and they were very peaceful. European settlement of Lenape land began more than fifty years before Penn's arrival in 1682. With these settlers came new diseases which killed many Lenape. Estimates vary, but it is believed that only 4000 Lenape had survived and still lived in what became Pennsylvania. Increased European settlement forced many Lenape from their homes. Some Lenape still live in Pennsylvania and New Jersey, but many traveled as far as Oklahoma and even Canada to build new lives.

WILLIAM PENN (1644–1718) was born in England. As a young man he joined the Society of Friends, or Quakers as most called them. His wealthy father, Admiral William Penn, loaned money to the King of England. When the Admiral died, the King repaid the loan by giving William a huge tract of land in the New World. The King named it *Pensilvania*, "Penn's Woods," in honor of the Admiral. Before coming to his Province, William Penn sent letters of peace to Lenape chiefs and negotiated many treaties with them. The Lenape called William Penn "Onas," their word for "pen."

Broomsticks in Pennsylvania

THREE HUNDRED YEARS ago, people talked a lot about witches. Not the make-believe witches in fairy tales and books. They talked about *real* people and accused them of doing evil and scary things.

These accusations could land a person into big trouble! Back in 1692 young girls pointed their fingers at hundreds of people in Salem, Massachusetts. During the Salem Witch Trials nineteen people were convicted of witchcraft and then hanged.

But this could never have happened in William Penn's peaceful province of Pennsylvania, could it?

Here's the surprise. It did!

It was back in 1683, and William Penn himself presided over Pennsylvania's first — and last — witch trial. According to English law, a person could be brought to court for "conjuration, witchcraft and dealing with evil and wicked spirits." Accused of *all* of that? Margaret Matson!

Margaret Matson was Swedish so she spoke . . . Swedish!

She was old and some people also accused her of being . . . REALLY ugly!

Poor Margaret. She *was* a bit different from most people. Rumors and accusations flew, then quicker than you could say, "abracadabra" . . .

Margaret Matson found herself in court.

There she faced a panel of judges which included the governor, William Penn.

Old, Swedish Margaret gave her plea.

"Not guilty!"

And with that, Margaret's trial began! She watched as the judge said,

> "Call the first witness to the stand. Henry Drystreet!"

Henry Drystreet walked to the stand. He looked at Margaret, then he gave his testimony.

> "Twenty years ago, someone told me . . . Margaret Matson is a witch! AND she bewitched several cows!"

Henry sat down. The judge said,

"Next witness! James Saunderling!"

James Saunderling took the stand and he said,

"My mother told me, Margaret Matson bewitched
a cow!"

A bewitched cow. *This* was a serious accusation. Back in
1683, before there were veterinarians, people tried to figure out
why a cow suddenly went dry and no longer produced milk.
Without the benefit of science, they concocted all kinds of
reasons, such as . . . bewitching cows!

Oh poor Margaret!

But then James added, *very* quietly,

"It was later found that this was not the case."

The next witness, Charles Ashcom, added his evidence.

"One night, Margaret's own daughter ran hastily to
me and described a vision she had just had of a great
light! And, an old woman with a knife in her hand!!
Standing at the foot of her bed!!!"

AGGGHHH!!!!

Margaret denied this story and asked,

> "If this were true, where is my daughter to speak these words for herself?"

Good question, some thought.

The final witness, Amnakey Coolin, took the stand. She began to speak.

> "My husband once was boiling the heart of a dead cow who was bewitched. He wanted to break any spell that would bewitch more cows. While he did this, Margaret Matson watched him!"

The judge asked,

> "And, did Margaret Matson say anything to your husband?"

The woman replied,

> "Yes, Margaret asked, 'What are you doing?' And my husband replied, 'I am boiling the heart of a bewitched cow to fix this curse.'"

> "And, did Margaret respond in any way?"

"She said, "it would be better to boil . . . the bones!"

AGGHHHH!!!!

Poor Margaret. Such accusations!

But defiantly, she denied them all and declared that the witnesses spoke "hear say!"

So, how did the court rule? And, what happened to Margaret?

As the judge and the Governor, William Penn might have made this decision alone. But, he wanted Pennsylvania to be a place where the rule of law was truly "of the people." Trial by jury, not trial by Governor, was his desire and the law of his province. This was a very new idea and set the precedent for our modern legal system.

So rather than rule himself, he charged the jury to reach its verdict.

As they deliberated, Margaret awaited her fate. Would they find her guilty . . . or not guilty? Would she live . . . or die?

At last the jury returned. Governor Penn asked,

"Have you reached a verdict?"

"We have, Governor Penn."

"What is the verdict?"

"We find that the accused, Margaret Matson is *guilty* of having the common fame of a witch but we find her *not guilty* in the manner and form as she stands indicted."

This meant that the jury agreed that Margaret might have the *reputation* of being a witch. But, they found her *not* guilty of witchcraft in the eyes of the law. So, Margaret was . . . free!

Or, *almost* free. She still had to pay a fine and assure her good behavior in the future. Which she did, for she never again faced charges of bewitching cows.

So ended the first — and last — trial for witchcraft in Pennsylvania. According to beloved legend, when asked about the case, William Penn reportedly said,

"In Pennsylvania, it is not against the law to ride a broomstick."

Margaret Matson and the Swedes

DUTCH AND SWEDISH settlers were the first Europeans to settle along the Delaware River in what became Pennsylvania, Delaware and New Jersey. The Swedes brought with them the tradition of building houses of logs — log cabins — which over time other Europeans adopted. Margaret Matson was one of about 2000 Swedish and Dutch people already in Pennsylvania when William Penn and his English Quaker settlers began arriving in 1681. Evidence of Philadelphia's Swedish roots survives in the city's flag which is light blue and yellow, just like the flag of Sweden.

Lydia Darragh: Quaker Spy

Sweet, demure Lydia Darragh was a Quaker . . .

She was a patriot . . .

And . . .

Lydia Darragh was a spy!

Lydia's espionage career began in 1777, just one year after Thomas Jefferson, Benjamin Franklin, and the other patriots had signed the Declaration of Independence. Things were not going well for the Americans. They had lost many battles to the British. Then, in September 1777, the British army captured Philadelphia!

To make bad matters even worse, the British commanding officer General William Howe, now lived in a house . . . *directly* across the street from Lydia.

One day, a British officer pounded on Lydia's door and demanded that she vacate her house. Lydia refused and then asked to speak to General Howe. He agreed to meet and the two struck a deal. Lydia and her family could remain in their house *IF* she let the British use it for meetings every now and then.

So, British officers occasionally met in Lydia's house.

This was fine, for a while. Then, everything changed on December 2, 1777. British Captain John André came to her house and told Lydia that General William Howe and some officers would meet that night in her house — in *private!* Then Captain André said,

> "And be sure, Lydia, that your family are all in bed at an early hour. I shall expect you to attend this request. When our guests are ready to leave the house, I will myself give you notice, that you may let us out, and extinguish the fire and candles."

Lydia agreed.

That night, she and her family retired to their chambers at 8 o'clock, leaving the British redcoats downstairs to conduct their business.

Lydia tossed and turned on her bed, wondering and worrying. Her son, Charles, was in George Washington's army, and she believed in the patriots' fight for freedom and independence. What if something important was happening downstairs, right in her own home?

She tossed and turned some more. Then she decided. Tonight, she thought,

> "Tonight I will do a bit of spying to see what those British soldiers might be planning!"

Lydia threw off her covers and took off her shoes. *Silently,* she crept outside her bed chamber. It was cold and dark. She was terrified. *Silently,* she crept downstairs to the room where the British officers were meeting. The door was closed. *Silently,* she put her ear to the key-hole . . .

. . . And she listened as the officers laid their plan for a surprise attack on the Americans, now camped outside the city in a small settlement called Whitemarsh. It was to be on . . .

December 4!

And this was the night of December 2!

Oh no! Lydia *knew* she had to get this information to General Washington. She also knew she had to return quickly to her chamber. She tiptoed back, she got into her bed, and she wondered, "What can I do?"

All of a sudden, someone pounded on her door! Lydia at first froze with fear, but then she collected herself and rose from her bed. She opened the door, stretching and rubbing her eyes as if she had been wakened from a deep sleep.

Captain John André stared at her.

Oh no, Lydia thought. Had he seen her? Or had he heard her as she knelt outside the meeting room door?

The Captain looked at her and said,

"Our meeting is concluded. We shall leave now."

Knees shaking, Lydia followed him downstairs and bid good night to the departing redcoats. She extinguished candles . . .

she crept back in the dark and cold to her chamber . . .

and she began to devise her plan . . .

The next morning Lydia went to British headquarters with a request.

"My family needs flour. I need to leave Philadelphia and go to the Frankfort Mill. Can I please have a pass so I can cross British lines?"

Lydia *looked* innocent enough. Or so thought the British soldier who handed her a pass signed by General Howe himself.

Holding the pass and an empty sack for the flour, Lydia walked out of Philadelphia.

Out past the redcoats guarding the city.

Out into the open countryside . . . which brought her closer and closer to the American lines.

With each step, Lydia knew she was about to commit a crime so serious, she could lose her life. With each step, she surely prayed she would succeed. . . .

Then at last she saw an American officer she knew. Lydia told him what she had heard and asked him to relay the information to General Washington. Then, she turned around and walked back to Philadelphia, carrying a bag filled with flour.

She entered her house, not knowing what might happen.

The next day, December 4, she listened as the battle drums beat and she watched the British army march out of the city . . . toward Whitemarsh!

Lydia prayed that her message had been delivered . . .

On December 5 Lydia got the answer to her prayer. The Americans had sprung their own surprise at Whitemarsh, greeting the British army with cannons and guns pointed right at them! The British had no choice but retreat back to Philadelphia.

But Lydia knew her ordeal was far from over. Several days later someone pounded on her door, furiously. As she rose to answer it, her heart pounded, just as furiously.

She opened the door, and Captain André *demanded* that she come with him — *immediately!* She followed him into the same room where the officers had met on December 2. He locked the door and told her to sit.

> "Were any of your family up, Lydia, on the night when I received company in this house?"

Lydia looked at the officer and without hesitation she replied,

> "No. They all retired at eight o'clock."

He looked at her carefully, then remembered how hard he had knocked that night in order to wake her so that she could let the officers out of the house. He stared at her.

> "One thing is certain. The enemy had notice of our coming, were prepared for us, and we marched back like a parcel of fools. The walls must have ears!"

What could Lydia do but nod and agree? Yes, surely it was the *walls* which must have ears!

Yes, Lydia Darragh later said to her children and her friends. It was those "walls" and their "ears" which hood-winked . . . the whole British army!

Lydia Darragh

LYDIA BARRINGTON DARRAGH (1729–1789) was born in Ireland and moved to Philadelphia shortly after she married William Darragh in 1753. She was a nurse and a midwife, and like Betsy Ross, was called a "Fighting Quaker" because she actively supported the Revolutionary War. (Most Quakers did not.) Lydia likely carried messages written on tiny pieces of papers which she hid inside of buttons and pouches, then delivered to Americans waiting for her outside the city. The story of her adventures in December 1777 first appeared in accounts written by her family and friends in the 1820s. The accounts have some differences in details, something that can happen when well-loved tales get told over the years. What remains unquestioned is the fact that Lydia Darragh was a spy, as recognized by the CIA, and her espionage helped disrupt the British plan for Whitemarsh.

General Howe and the Cow

BACK IN 1777, America and England were busy fighting a Revolution, and Pennsylvania was in the thick of the battle. But this story isn't about battles. This story is about the single biggest problem an army can face — feeding the army! As some wise soldier once said, an army marches on its stomach, and if stomachs aren't full, that army won't work very well.

And, in 1777 there were two *very* hungry armies camped in and around Philadelphia. There was the British Army with about 15,000 soldiers led by General William Howe. They had marched in and captured Philadelphia, and now they settled into warm, cozy brick houses, happy to wait out the winter.

Out in the country, there was the American army led by General George Washington. He and about 12,000 soldiers settled into winter quarters on the hills of Valley Forge. They lived in huts, not warm, cozy brick houses.

With these two armies camped in Philadelphia and Valley Forge, there were now close to 30,000 *extra* mouths to feed in this part of Pennsylvania. This in addition to the many hungry Pennsylvanians who already lived here.

Oh, so many mouths to feed!

But, it just so happened that Pennsylvania had lots of farms which produced lots of food, and some farmers sized up the situation.

"Ah ha!" they thought. "With all these people to feed, we can make money selling food! Those armies will pay us lots of money for our pigs, wheat, and vegetables!"

So, some Pennsylvania farmers sold food to the Americans. Some sold it to the British. Some sold to *both* armies.

And lots of other hungry Pennsylvanians? Well, they tried to *hide* their food from *both* armies, which got pretty desperate for food at times.

Even when food was short, both General Howe and General Washington tried to prevent their soldiers from stealing it. They knew, though, that *sometimes* their soldiers would have to *forage* for food. Forage. That means go out and *look* for food. Not *steal* food, right. . . . ?

But every now and then, General Howe or General Washington had to address this issue of — *foraging*. Some Pennsylvanians defined this word a bit differently. They defined it as — *s-t-e-a-l-i-n-g*. These Pennsylvanians got angry, so they marched themselves over to their local headquarters and filed their complaints.

One of these people was Jane Gibbons. Jane was seventy-five years old and she was very proper. She wore simple clothes because she was a Quaker and she also used the Quaker style of language which was a bit different from what most people used at that time. Proper Quaker Jane was quite upset because her favorite cow had disappeared, and she was *quite* sure the British army had *s-t-o-l-e-n* her. Because Jane was so highly respected, the British granted her permission to see their commander — General William Howe himself.

Off she marched to British headquarters. She rapped on the door and when a British soldier opened it she said,

> "Good day, friend. My name is Jane Gibbons. I have come to see General Howe about my cow."

With a few more words of explanation, the soldier took Jane to General William Howe. She looked the commander squarely in the eye and asked,

> "General Howe, hast thou seen my cow?"

The General looked at proper Quaker Jane and responded,

> "I have heard you lost your cow. I am sorry to hear that, madam. But as you know, I have instructed my

soldiers to refrain from stealing food or animals from our *loyal* Pennsylvanians. State your name please."

"My name is Jane Gibbons."

"Have you not a son in the *rebel* army?"

Rebel army. That's what the British called the Americans. Rebels.

"Yes, sir, I have a son in *George Washington's* army."

That Jane is a clever one isn't she? See how she avoided saying *rebel* army? But back to headquarters.

"I am afraid, madam, that you love your *cow* better than your *king!*"

Oh no! General Howe was *not* happy with Jane and things looked grim for her cow.

What could Jane do?

This may surprise you, but here's what she *really* said in that meeting with General Howe,

"I bid thee farewell."

And with that, Jane Gibbons left General Howe — *without* her cow.

Oh no! But what about Jane's cow? What happened to her?

Well, Jane Gibbons' cow clearly had the last laugh over General Howe. Years later her family proudly recorded that their good Quaker cow "escaped from the enemy and found her way back to her kind mistress."

What they *never* said was whether she *might* have gotten just a *little* help along the way. What do *you* think?

That, my friends, is the true story of General Howe and the Cow.

Jane Gibbons

JANE GIBBONS was a member of a large and prominent Quaker family who lived near Westtown, in Chester County, Pennsylvania. Colonel William Gibbons, son of Jane Gibbons, was the commander of the 7th Battalion of the Chester County Militia, which in General Howe's eyes, made him a member of the "rebel" American army. Quakers believe in pacifism, so most did not serve during the Revolution, but some, like Colonel Gibbons, did join the army.

The Battle of the Kegs

Gallants, attend, and hear a friend
Trill forth harmonious ditty,
Strange things I'll tell that late befell
In Philadelphia city.

MOST BATTLES take place on battlefields. But *sometimes* there are battles which are just a little different. . . .

Like the Battle of the Kegs!

The story begins in the summer of 1777. That's when General William Howe, commander of the British Army, decided to capture Philadelphia. He thought,

Seize Philadelphia! Capture that city where those rebels wrote that Declaration of Independence!

That would end this nasty little Revolutionary War!

First, though, he had to get his troops out of New York City. He had two options.

He could sail.

Or, he could *mostly* march.

Normally, the fastest route was by water. If he put his troops on ships, they could sail south on the Atlantic Ocean, until they reached the Chesapeake Bay. They could head up the Bay, then sail in triumph right up the Delaware River.

But General Howe knew he had one *big* problem — Fort Mifflin, which sat on lovely Mud Island, right in the middle of the Delaware River, just south of Philadelphia. Inside, armed American troops waited. Outside, armed ships of the Pennsylvania Navy waited.

Then there was the *other* problem — the *chevaux de frises.* These were thick, square timbers with sharp iron tips which the Americans had sunk into the riverbed. If a British ship ripped its hull on one of those? That would be *very* bad, and the General knew he could not take that risk.

So General Howe chose to *mostly* march his way to Philadelphia. After sailing to Maryland, his redcoats left their ships and set out into the hot, steamy American weather. Besides pesky mosquitoes, they faced lots of pesky Americans ready to fight.

The two armies battled at Brandywine and skirmished here and there, but in late September it was over. General Howe and the British army marched in and captured Philadelphia!

Now General Howe turned his attention to the Delaware River. He needed to capture Fort Mifflin so British ships could bring food and other supplies into Philadelphia.

He gave orders to the British.

"Ready, aim, fire!"

And they did, right at the Fort!

For six weeks, British cannons hurled more than 10,000 cannonballs at Fort Mifflin and the American soldiers inside. The cannon fire was so loud that General Washington heard it many miles away. At last, on November 15 the remaining Americans evacuated the Fort, leaving the red, white and blue striped Continental flag still flying.

With the Fort captured, British ships now carefully dodged the *chevaux de frises* and brought supplies into Philadelphia.

Not long after, General Washington settled into his chilly winter quarters in Valley Forge. There he could keep an eye on the British, but also, *maybe,* make their stay in Philadelphia just a *little* more difficult. . . .

He thought,

Hmmm. It's time for something a little bit...clever and ingenious!

Something that will surprise those smug redcoats . . .

General Washington looked around, and then he found *just* the man for the job.

David Bushnell! Inventor of . . . The American Torpedo!!

General Washington wasn't thinking about the Torpedo for this particular assignment. He didn't need a submarine which looked like a turtle — *that* was the Torpedo. He needed . . .

Floating combustibles!

What a great idea!

So great that David Bushnell had to figure out what a floating combustible *was*.

Good thing David was an inventor, because he came up with a clever and ingenious solution. He needed something that would float and combust — meaning BLOW UP!

So he came up with a formula rather like this:

To Make Floating Combustible

Take One Barrel or Keg, preferably very large. Fill to bursting with explosives. Seal. Float down Delaware River. Let bob until hits large British ship . . . and . . . then . . . wait . . . ker-BLAM!.

David and his helpers filled barrels and kegs with explosives, creating a whole *squadron* of floating combustibles.

Then, one night, David set them adrift . . .

Off they floated . . .

down the Delaware . . .

    right . . .

        for . . .

All those British ships bobbing up and down so happily on the Delaware River!

Then . . .

    suddenly . . .

        one ship . . . *Blew* UP!

✸ *BAM! POW! ker-BLAM!* ✸

And with that, British soldiers started leaping out of their beds! They were under attack!

Redcoats piled out onto the river bank and wharves. They aimed their guns and cannons . . . at . . . what was that out there?

Barrels? Barrels out there, bobbing down the Delaware, right near their ships!

What, they think???

Not wanting to take any chances (there might be Americans hiding in those barrels, after all!), they steadied their guns . . .

    Then, ready . . .

        They aimed. . . .

            And they . . . FIRED!

✸ *Ka-BOOM!* ✸

They fired again! And there were more BOOMS as floating combustibles combusted and blew up out there on the River! Talk about a battle!!!

But here's why this battle was just a bit different, because that's about *all* that happened. Just one British ship sank and there was not an American in sight. Eventually the red-faced redcoats realized they have been had — by a bunch of barrels!

Back in Valley Forge George Washington's troops heard about this battle which didn't happen on a battlefield. They laughed and even sang about their victory in

The Battle of the Kegs!

'Twas early day, as poets say,
Just when the sun was rising,
A soldier stood on log of wood
And saw a sight surprising.

As, in amaze, he stood to gaze;
The truth can't be denied, sirs,
He spied a score of kegs or more,
Come floating down the tide, sirs.

A sailor, too, in jerkin blue,
The strange appearance viewing,
First damned his eyes in great surprise,
Then said, "Some mischief's brewing."

Francis Hopkinson

FRANCIS HOPKINSON, a Signer of the Declaration of Independence, was also a poet with a wicked sense of humor. He wrote a song, "The Battle of the Kegs," which Americans sang to the tune "Yankee Doodle." Some of his verses are in the story!

Rebecca Franks, Tory Teen
and Party Queen

READY FOR a little romance? A little music? A little *scandal*? Let's go back to May 18, 1778 and go to . . . the *Mischianza!*

The Mischia-whatsa?

The *Mischianza!* (*Misk-ee-*AHN-*za!*) That's a fake Italian word for the most amazing ball ever held in Philadelphia. It was an evening filled with romance, music, candles, flowing gowns, jousting, feasting!

And, enough scandal to make tongues wag for *hundreds* of years.

And the belle of this ball? None other than the lovely Rebecca Franks! Eighteen-year old Rebecca was the youngest child of Margaret and David Franks. Her father was a merchant who made a fortune by trading with *good* old Mother England. So, in 1778, when Rebecca Franks found herself in the midst of this little *disruption* . . . this Revolution . . . it was clear that . . .

Rebecca Franks was *not* a patriot. She was a Loyalist, a Tory. She *loved* Mother England. *Loved* those British soldiers who had captured Philadelphia in September 1777. All those soldiers were living in people's homes, walking on the streets, shopping, going to the theater, and oh, occasionally doing battle.

And Rebecca? Well, she spent the fall and winter of 1777 and 1778 doing what girls love to do. Dark-haired, lovely, she gossiped with her friends,

> "All those *handsome* soldiers. Oh, such a charming
> fix we are in, ladies! Don't you *love* their *red*
> uniforms?"

All those British soldiers. All these lovely Philadelphia ladies. And, by March 1778, not a battle in sight. One brave man stepped into the breach to save one and all — from utter boredom!

> "Let's have a ball, a *Mischianza*!" Captain John
> André declared.

The Captain laid his battle plan. First, he raised money from his fellow officers — over 3300 guineas, a tremendous amount of money and enough to feed the Americans camped at Valley Forge for weeks. It was also enough to underwrite a party for the . . . *ages.*

His theme? The Middle Ages! At his *Mischianza,* brave British knights would vie for the hearts of beautiful princesses, *Philadelphia* princesses.

Among the Philadelphia princesses? The lovely Rebecca Franks.

The British soldiers worked on costumes and decorations for two months. The Philadelphia Princesses drank tea, gossiped, and practiced dancing for two months. Then at last, the big day arrived! So now, let's join Rebecca on her big night. . . .

It's May 18, 1778. Rebecca is primping. She slips on a flowing white silk dress, cut low. She ties her lovely sash, trimmed with spangles. And her hair, her glorious hair! Her hairdresser combs, teases, and *rats* her hair as high as it can go. (No, the hairdresser does not put rats in her hair. That's the word they used back then for teasing.)

Rebecca tops her ratted hair with a turban. Then, carefully, she pins on a *favor* — a fancy decoration she will bestow upon the knight who wins her heart. She sighs,

"Oh heart, be still!"

One look in the looking glass . . . oh, perfection!

It's nearly 4:30 — time to go! Rebecca gets her ticket which she needs to get in. This is an exclusive party after all! She leaves her house, steps in her coach, then heads down to the Delaware River where she sees a parade of ships and boats, all decorated with streamers and flags. And there is music! What's that they are playing? Why it's . . . *God Save the King!*

Rebecca steps, oh so daintily, onto her galley. (That's a fancy word for rowboat.) She takes a seat, and lots of *strong* British sailors row the galley down the Delaware. Rebecca waves to lots of people standing on the banks of the River, watching this spectacle.

Then, all of a sudden BOOM! Gunfire! Cannons! The mighty British warship, the *Roebuck,* fires its salute to Rebecca and the other Philadelphia Princesses. They exclaim,

"Those cannons are firing . . . For us!"

Rebecca flits her fan and fixes her hair as the galley slips into the dock at Walnut Grove. She and the Princesses are so excited as they chatter among themselves,

"Such a lovely estate for a ball!"

"Look at all the beautiful decorations!"

"Ooooooh, I hope my turban is on straight!"

Carefully, but gracefully, Rebecca steps off the galley and walks up a path lined with British soldiers. She flits her fan flirtatiously.

"Ooooooh, such tall, handsome soldiers!"

She passes beneath two triumphal arches and enters a pavilion. She takes a seat in the front and waits for the festivities to begin.

Out in the center of the pavilion dashing knights sit on their noble steeds, eager to vie for the hearts of the Princesses.

Rebecca and some of her friends are Princesses of the Burning Mountain. Witty, beautiful, accomplished!

Across the way are more friends of hers, Princesses of the Blended Rose. Also witty, beautiful, and accomplished!

Rebecca flits her fan then smiles at the Knights of the Burning Mountain, so handsome in their orange and black silk costumes.

"Oh heart, be still!"

Captain Watson approaches and bows to Princess Rebecca! The Captain is the chief of the Burning Mountain and he wears his symbol — a heart with a wreath of flowers. His motto? *Love and Glory!*

Rebecca and the Princesses are honored. Let the joust begin! The knights in their flowing silks, seize their lances and charge! The Princesses flit their fans with excitement.

> "Look at our knights, how they charge and salute.
> Ladies, have you ever seen such a spectacle?"

At last the knights cease their knightly labors and the fair Princesses reward them with a gift. Rebecca unpins the *favor* from her turban and presents it to Captain Watson.

> "Sir?"

> "Fair Princess!"

Ah, *Love and Glory!*

Night falls and at long last it is midnight. The handsome knights escort the Princesses into a tent filled with candles and hundreds of looking glasses *borrowed* from the homes of Philadelphians.

The supper table groans with 1200 delectable dishes. The guests feel thrilled and honored to be part of this magical night, but it is Rebecca and the Princesses who reign as the belles of the ball. They toast the King! They toast the Royal Family! And the merry *Mischianza* lasts 'til the sun rises. Only then will Rebecca and the Princesses return to their homes and take off their turbans.

Ah, the *Mischianza!* Truly an evening Rebecca Franks will never forget!

Fact is, Philadelphia never forgot the *Mischianza* either. Tongues wagged.

> The lavish expense? A *scandal!*
> Those low cut dresses? A *scandal!*
> Those *borrowed* looking glasses? A *scandal!*

Then there were people like American General Anthony Wayne who had spent the winter at Valley Forge. People called him "Mad" Anthony, and he was *mad,*

> "Dancing with the British? A *SCANDAL!!!!*"

Mad Anthony didn't stop there. After helping win an American victory in the Battle of Monmouth — just one month after the Mischianza — he declared,

> "Tell those Philadelphia ladies who attended . . .
> that the heavenly, sweet, pretty redcoats . . . have
> been humbled on the plains of Monmouth. The
> knights of the Blended Roses, and of the Burning
> Mount — have resigned their laurels to rebel

officers, who will lay them at the feet of those virtuous daughters of America who cheerfully gave up ease and affluence in a city, for liberty and peace of mind in a cottage."

As one of *those Philadelphia ladies* who attended the *Mischianza,* Rebecca Franks had charted her future. She and her family followed the British army to New York, and in 1782, she married British General Henry Johnson. With the war over in 1783 — the Americans beat the British! — they moved to England. With that, Rebecca Franks of Philadelphia became *Lady* Rebecca Johnson. But, when she was very old, she told an American visitor,

> "I have gloried in my rebel countrymen! Would to God, I, too, had been a patriot!"

Alas, Rebecca Franks had been a Princess, and *not* a Patriot, for she had danced at the magical and scandalous *Mischianza.*

Rebecca Franks

REBECCA FRANKS (c.1760–1823) was the third daughter and youngest of five children of David Franks (1720–1793) and his wife Margaret Evans (1720–1780). David Franks was born in New York City and was the son of Bilhah Abigail Levy Franks and Jacob Franks, a wealthy Jewish merchant who was also the Crown's agent for North America. When David moved to Philadelphia in 1740 he helped form a *minyan* where fellow Jews could worship together. David's wife Margaret was a member of Christ Church and three of their five children were baptized there. There is no record of baptism for Rebecca but it is likely that the Franks children were raised as Anglicans.

Allen McLane: Master Spy

DATELINE: VALLEY FORGE. June 16, 1778. General George Washington needs important information. Immediately. Are the British about to leave Philadelphia?

He knows just the man for the job.

McLane. Allen McLane. Captain Allen McLane. . . .

Master Spy!

Captain Allen McLane was a great soldier who fought hard in battles. But his real talent?

Moving swiftly and silently through the countryside . . .

gathering information . . .

swapping messages, finding food. . . .

And generally, wreaking as much havoc as possible. All for a good cause, of course.

For example, the Captain loved to intercept *certain* Pennsylvania farmers as they headed toward Philadelphia, their wagons groaning with food which they planned to sell — to the British!

Captain McLane would hide and wait, and when he saw one of those farmers, out he would jump! Then he would say something like,

> "Halt, Farmer! Hand over that food! We are taking it right back to where it's needed. To Valley Forge!"

Which Captain McLane then did.

Fun as that was, Captain McLane enjoyed dashing around the countryside even more. He captured a few British soldiers, he routinely warned the Americans about imminent attacks, he miraculously escaped various ambushes, all while doing what good spies do — remaining as invisible as possible. He also had a knack for being in just the right place at just the right time.

One of those right times occurred late on the night of May 18, 1778. Down on the Delaware River, the British army was throwing the biggest party Philadelphia had ever seen. They called it the *Mischianza* — a fancy name for a very fancy party. British soldiers and lovely Philadelphia ladies danced the night away in candlelit tents and enjoyed *delicious* food and lots of flirting.

As the partygoers danced, Captain McLane saw a *delicious* opportunity to wreak a bit of his trademark havoc . . .

So, with about 100 soldiers, he silently crept toward the city, closer and closer toward the British outposts guarding it. . . .

As lovely music played in the party tents, McLane gave the signal.

 ✸ *BOOM!* ✸

His men fired their rifles!

Next, they quickly poured whale oil over the sharp wooden spikes protecting the British entrenchments just outside the city. Then they set the spikes on fire, creating quite a blaze.

Amidst all this commotion, British pickets guarding the city scrambled for their guns. Was this a surprise American attack?

To find out, some British soldiers leapt onto horses and gave chase.

Captain McLane and his Americans obliged, leading the British redcoats on a merry ride through the countryside. They all even took a little swim in the Schuylkill River. Finally, the Captain turned the tables and chased the redcoats right back into Philadelphia.

Talk about a way to wreck a party!

It was one month after the *Mischianza* exploit that General Washington called on Captain McLane for a potentially dangerous and even deadly mission.

It all began when a young girl slipped through British lines into the American camp at Valley Forge. She found Captain McLane and gave him a note written by her father. The letter said the man would personally hand over intelligence which would aid the American cause. But there was a demand.

The man required a rendezvous . . . with Allen McLane . . . on the very next day.

Captain McLane and General Washington wondered, did this man know something that would help the American cause? Maybe something about the British leaving Philadelphia? That would be very useful information.

But, what if the letter was actually a clever trap, designed to capture America's most clever spy, Captain Allen McLane?

Knowing the risk, General Washington and Captain McLane agreed to meet the demand. So. . . .

Fearless as always, the Captain rode out of Valley Forge before dawn on June 16, 1778. He headed for the Horse House Tavern.

Smart as always, he took precautions. His entire troop followed at a safe distance, then hid behind the tavern.

The Captain approached the tavern, to all eyes, alone. A man waited inside the yard. He began to talk, so the Captain dismounted to hear what he was saying.

Suddenly, thirteen British soldiers galloped out on their horses, straight for the Captain!

Oh no! Was Allen McLane a goner?

Hardly.

The Captain leapt right back on his horse. Then he headed straight for a British soldier who had dismounted to open a gate.

The Captain reared his horse!

Then, he fired a pistol, right into the British soldier's face. One down, he thought.

But there were still all those other British soldiers, so the Captain knew he was not yet out of the woods.

But *back* in the woods, the sound of gunfire alerted his backup American troops. They raced *to* the scene, and suddenly it was the British who were outnumbered! So, those redcoats hastily galloped right on *out* of the scene.

With that, and yet again, Master Spy Captain Allen McLane escaped capture.

Two days later, on June 18, 1778, the Captain rode into Philadelphia. From the city he scribbled a note to his general back in Valley Forge. Upon reading the Captain's letter, General Washington added a note to one he was writing to Congress:

A letter from Captain McLane, dated in Philadelphia, this minute came to hand confirming the evacuation.

The British had left Philadelphia! General Washington and his army could now leave Valley Forge and reclaim the city where the Declaration of Independence had been written just two years before.

Philadelphia never again fell into British hands. And neither did Allen McLane!

Allen McLane

ALLEN MCLANE (1746–1829) was born in Philadelphia, then moved to Delaware in 1774 where he lived for the rest of his life. His family was well-off, but McLane exhausted his fortune during the Revolution. Someone once described Allen McLane as "a good hater." He was passionate, despised the British, loved warfare, and adored intrigue. He served in the Continental army from 1775 when he enlisted as a volunteer in Virginia, and his service ended in Virginia in 1781 where he was part of the American army which received the surrender of Lord Cornwallis at Yorktown. At the age of 68, Allen McLane commanded the defenses of Wilmington, Delaware during the War of 1812. General Washington once remarked to a friend about McLane: "I would not do without him in the light corps — no, not for a thousand pounds."

The Day
Charles Willson Peale
Almost Blew Up
Philadelphia

When the new United States at last signed a peace treaty with England on September 3, 1783, the new United States Congress made a great decision. All those Founders put their heads together and said,

"Let's Celebrate!"

And, to be sure this was not your usual, oh so proper silk, satin, and lace event, they hired the best party planner in town. . . .

Charles Willson Peale! Painter. Patriot. And Party Planner Extraordinaire!

Congress gave Charles £600 which was a LOT of money back then. Everyone wanted this to be a celebration Philadelphians would long remember.

Money in hand, Charles Willson Peale rolled up his sleeves. He put on his party planning thinking cap. He scratched his head. He thought some more. And then, he had it!

> "I will build a set of Roman arches, 56 feet wide, and they will stretch all the way across Market Street!"

Market Street is a *very* wide street in Philadelphia, so those Roman arches were a *very* big start for the *very* big party.

Those arches, though, were just the beginning, because Charles Willson Peale intended to create *magic* on Market Street. He thought some more, he scratched his head some more, and then he had it!

> "I will get lots of paper and I will paint some scenes from our Revolution. Then, I will hang those scenes between those arches I just put up on Market Street!"

Which he did!

Then, he had another great idea as he looked at the paper. It was translucent which meant he could see through it when he held it up to a light. Hmmm, he thought.

"Maybe I can put a light behind the paintings and make them *glow!*"

But, how to do it? He looked around . . . And, then he found . . . 1150 lamps! Not electric lamps since there was no electricity back in January 1784. These were lamps lit with oil. When he put those 1150 lamps behind the paintings done on translucent paper . . . it was magic! The paintings glowed!

The arches, the paintings on translucent paper, and the lamps — all this was good. But, to make it even better? Charles Willson Peale put on his inventor's cap again, he scratched his head again, and then he had it!

"I will make these glowing paintings . . . *move!*"

So he invented some mechanical devices which made it look like the scenes in the paintings moved.

One moving painting showed American Indians, *building* a church in the wilderness. Another showed George Washington and American patriots *whupping* the British redcoats.

It was spectacular! It was glorious! It was like the movies, only this was January 1784 and nobody had ever heard of movies!

But as spectacular as this was, Charles Willson Peale saved the very best for the very last. After all, a party to celebrate the new nation and the new peace with England required something big. *Really* big. So Charles thought some more, he scratched his head some more, and then he had it.

"I will build a *colossal* figure and call her — *Peace!*"

Which he did!

Now he needed a place to perch his *Peace*. He looked up and down Market Street, and focused on a grand house occupied by Pennsylvania's Governor.

"Perfect," he thought, so he put *Peace* up on the Governor's roof. She had a great view of Philadelphia!

Then, Charles put on his thinking cap one more time and scratched his head one last time.

> "This big statue of *Peace* is great, and she looks beautiful up there on the roof, but if I can make those moving pictures move, maybe I can make *her* move too . . . and . . . I know! Maybe *Peace* can *light* all those 1150 lamps!"

So, that's what he did!

To start, he tied some ropes around *Peace*. Then, he lowered her, oh so gently, from the roof. Next he figured out a way to make it *look* like she was lighting a fuse. Then this fuse would light . . . all 1150 lamps! Once those lamps were lit, the magic would begin! Charles was so excited.

"The transparencies will *glow!* The machines will make them *move!* And, Washington and all the American patriots will *whup* the English, yet again!"

And, for the crowning touch to this already spectacular event?

Fireworks! That's right, 700 rockets erupting from the top of that Roman arch stretching 56 feet over Market Street.

Talk about a night to remember . . . !

The thing was, folks remembered that night for slightly different reasons from what Charles Willson Peale intended.

It all began when he lit those fuses surrounded by all those fireworks . . .

Suddenly, sparks flew! They sprayed out over the crowds — and all over Charles Willson Peale, standing proudly atop his grand Roman arch. Then, the arch burst into flames! Charles scrambled down from his perch, only to find himself in the line of fire, coming not from his painted British redcoats, but from dozens of exploding rockets which burned his head and hands, and set his clothes ablaze.

Though he survived, two people died, and in ten short minutes, his entire creation burned to a crisp. . . .

After this celebration which everyone remembered for all the wrong reasons, Charles Willson Peale hung up his party planning hat. He shifted to less explosive activities, such as creating the Philadelphia Museum. He filled it with portraits

of the patriots, lots of stuffed dead birds and animals, and most amazing of all, a *colossal* skeleton of a prehistoric creature — a mighty Mammoth!

But why not his *colossal* statue of *Peace?*

Alas, poor *Peace.* She was no longer available.

Charles Willson Peale

A SHORT BIOGRAPHY cannot do justice to the life of the highly creative and hugely productive Charles Willson Peale (1741–1827). He was born in Maryland where he learned the crafts of watchmaking, silversmithing, upholstery, and sign painting. He settled on painting after training with two famous American artists, John Singleton Copley and Benjamin West. Peale moved to Philadelphia in 1776, a momentous year in the largest city of the American colonies. He was a patriot and he served in the Continental army. He sketched and painted many of the officers who also served. Later he created large portraits of these Founders which he hung in his Philadelphia Museum. Many of these paintings hang today in the Second Bank of the United States in Philadelphia.

Escape From the President's House: The Amazing Story of Oney Judge

PHILADELPHIA WAS THE CAPITAL of the United States from 1790 until 1800, so President George Washington lived here along with his family from 1790 until 1797. The President's House once stood at the corner of Sixth and Market Streets, and during the summer of 2007, archaeologists excavated its site.

Such amazing discoveries hid beneath layers of soil!

> Foundation walls of the house . . .
> Broken bits of china used by the Washingtons. . . .
> Even the foundation for a large oval-shaped window
> which President Washington added to the main

parlor. This was the model for the Oval Office in the next President's House — the White House!

The archaeologists also discovered foundations for kitchen walls, stable walls, and the remains of an underground walkway which connected the grand main house with these spaces.

Long ago, these spaces hummed with activity. For it was here that indentured servants and enslaved people did their essential work to maintain the Washington household.

Oney Judge was one of these people. She was born at President Washington's plantation, Mount Vernon in about 1773. In 1796, when she was about twenty-three, President Washington himself described Oney,

> "She has been a particular attendant on Mrs.
> Washington since she was ten years old; and she was
> handy and useful to her, being a perfect Mistress of
> her needle."

Skilled seamstress, personal servant to Martha Washington . . . No wonder that the President and Mrs. Washington brought Oney with them from Mount Vernon, first to New York City, and then to Philadelphia.

Imagine what Oney thought when she left the only home she had known, a big plantation in the country, where people she loved also lived. Then, imagine what Oney thought when she arrived in Philadelphia, the biggest and most populous city in the new United States! It was oh, so different from Mount Vernon in oh, so many ways! And, for her, the biggest way?

In Philadelphia Oney found herself surrounded by a community of people who were black, just like her! But these people were free, and she was not.

These free Philadelphians of color were active citizens in the new country. They had founded important institutions — churches, schools, and organizations which helped the community. They worked for wages which they kept. They had families. They were ministers, and seamstresses, and laundresses and business owners like James Forten, who built a fortune in his sailmaking business where he employed both black and white workers.

Oney must have shaken her head and marveled, "These people are like me, but they are FREE!"

Oney quickly made friends with these free people of color. As they talked, a plan for Oney's future grew. For having seen this freedom, Oney wanted to be free, too. With all her heart, she did not want to remain in slavery. She also feared that her masters were about to give her — as a wedding present — to Martha Washington's granddaughter.

Give her away!

Oney knew what she had to do. She had to escape! Escape from the President of the United States himself! And, escape from the President's own house!

67

So, one night in the spring of 1796, Oney made her move . . .

"Whilst they were packing up to go to Virginia, I was packing to go, I didn't know where; for I knew that if I went back to Virginia, I should never get my liberty. I had friends among the colored people of Philadelphia, had my things carried there beforehand, and left Washington's house while they were eating dinner."

Plain and simple, as the President dined, Oney crept out of the house. She slipped outside and then she hid with some of her friends in Philadelphia. Somehow, someone found a ship, sailing north. Somehow, Oney got on board and left the city. She left everything she knew and everyone who knew her, including the President of the United States!

Oney sailed farther and farther north, at last landing in Portsmouth, New Hampshire . . .

Meanwhile, back in Philadelphia, the President and Mrs. Washington wondered,

"Where is Oney?"

At first they thought,

"A French man has lured her away!"

Oh no!

But *then* they realized,

> "Oney has escaped! On her *own!*"

Martha Washington was outraged! How could this girl who lived in her house be so ungrateful and run away? She urged the President,

> "Place an ad in the paper! Offer a reward to the person who returns Oney!"

The President wisely refused. He knew this would anger many Philadelphians. So, he put his Secretary of the Treasury on the case. Through friends and government connections, Joseph Whipple of New Hampshire at last located Oney and spoke with her. He reported back to the President,

> *"After a cautious examination it appeared to me that she had not been decoyed away by a Frenchman as had been apprehended, but that a thirst for compleat freedom which she was informed would take place on her arrival here . . . had been her only motive for absconding . . ."*

No, a French man had not lured her away. It was Oney's thirst for complete freedom which sent her on her journey. It was so strong she resisted all additional efforts by the Washingtons to get her to return. She did this well knowing that she could be captured and returned to slavery because of the Fugitive Slave Law, which President Washington had signed in Philadelphia.

But, this never happened! Instead, Oney Judge lived out her long life in New Hampshire. She married, she had children, she had friends who loved her, and when needed, friends who hid her so that she could remain in her new home. Shortly before she died at the ripe old age of 75, someone asked Oney if she ever regretted leaving the Washingtons. She replied simply,

"No, I am free . . ."

Oney Judge

ONA (ONEY) JUDGE was born a slave in about 1773 at Mount Vernon. She was the daughter of Betty, a seamstress, and Andrew White, a white English tailor who worked as an indentured servant. As a young girl Oney moved into the Washingtons' home to be the playmate for Nelly Custis, Martha Washington's granddaughter. Later she became a personal servant to Mrs. Washington. Oney accompanied President Washington to New York City in 1789 and then to Philadelphia in 1790 when the national capital moved there. While in Philadelphia, President Washington signed the Fugitive Slave Law of 1793. This law stated that slaveholders had the right to reclaim slaves who had escaped. By 1796, Oney was one of three slaves living at the President's House. The others were Moll and Hercules, the cook. Hercules also escaped to freedom. Once in New Hampshire, Oney married John Staines of Portsmouth. They had three children. As an old woman, Oney told her story to abolitionists who eagerly published it as part of their crusade to end slavery in the United States.

Up, Up & Away

THE WRIGHT BROTHERS are famous for flying the first successful airplane, and Neil Armstrong made history as the first man to set foot on the moon. But, another man beat all three on January 9, 1793. Newspapers called him a "bold AERONAUT" for he was about to fly high above Philadelphia.

His name? Monsieur Jean-Pierre Blanchard. Jean-Pierre came from France to do something so astonishing that President George Washington took time away from his Presidential duties to witness it.

The bold aeronaut's journey had begun ten years before, in 1783, when Jean-Pierre witnessed a most amazing spectacle. In his native country of France, two brothers — the Montgolfiers — invented and created a hot air balloon. They tested it, and it flew! Then they sent up another balloon carrying animals as passengers. It flew too! Most thrillingly, in

November 1783, two men got into a Montgolfier balloon. Up they flew, the first men to soar the skies!

Down below, Benjamin Franklin watched these balloon experiments with great excitement. He was in France to work out a peace treaty between England and the new United States. Alas, he knew he was too old to fly. But that other witness, Jean-Pierre? He was much younger and he knew he wanted to fly too!

So, he did!

Between 1784 and 1792, Jean-Pierre made forty-four flights. His most famous journey occurred when he flew across the English Channel with an American doctor. They nearly crashed and died, but they made it. When they landed in France, they delivered a letter they had carried — the first air mail delivery in history!

Now, in 1793, Jean-Pierre was ready for his forty-fifth flight, this time, in the New World. He chose his launch pad, Philadelphia, the capital of the new United States and also its biggest city. But Philadelphia was also William Penn's "Greene Countrie Towne" which meant that there were trees everywhere. And where there weren't trees, there were buildings! Where could he launch his balloon safely?

He looked and looked and at last Jean-Pierre found the perfect place — prison! Specifically, the Yard of the Walnut Street Prison, which stood very near the Pennsylvania State House, now called Independence Hall.

Jean-Pierre set about making his hot air balloon, stitching

together hundreds of yards of yellow silk. He attached the balloon with ropes to the wicker "boat" where he would ride. He would inflate his balloon with hot air produced by a fire. Once inflated, his balloon would . . . Fly!

At last the momentous day arrived. At 9 a.m. on that cold, crisp January morning, several thousand spectators crowded the prison yard, eager to witness history. They listened as a band played solemn music while Jean-Pierre began inflating his balloon. Slowly, the balloon changed shape from limp silk to a growing golden ball stretching, reaching, pushing up to the sky. The crowd watched in awe, and perhaps just a little terror.

Then at the stroke of 10, Jean-Pierre accepted a letter from President Washington and he bid *adieu* to the spectators. Wearing a plain blue suit and a cocked hat adorned with jaunty feathers, he leaped into the blue wicker boat. Once settled inside, he threw out some ballast — heavy weights. Then, slowly . . . the golden balloon began to rise. Jean-Pierre called out,

"*Au revoir,* Philadelphia! Good-bye!"

Jean-Pierre waved the flags of the United States and France as he drifted off, going . . . where?

He floated above the city, and watched people get

smaller

and smaller

and smaller.

Buildings that were big on the ground suddenly looked tiny. Christ Church, the Pennsylvania State House, busy Market Street, *au revoir!*

His golden balloon headed south and several men on horseback tried to keep up. They gave up, though, because it traveled too fast — a speedy 20 miles an hour!

Jean-Pierre passed over the Delaware River. *Au revoir,* Pennsylvania!

Then, *Bonjour* and Hello, New Jersey!

After flying for forty-six minutes, Jean-Pierre landed fifteen miles from his starting place, near the town of Woodbury, New Jersey. He held the folded paper which President Washington had given to him. It was America's first air mail delivered letter. Inside, the President's words suited the historic occasion for in it he declared,

> *To all citizens of the United States, and others, that in his passage, descent, return or journeying elsewhere, . . . to the said Mr. Blanchard . . . receive and aid him with that humanity and good will, which may render honor to their country, and justice to an individual so distinguished by his efforts to establish and advance an art, in order to make it useful to mankind in general.*

Later in the day Jean-Pierre returned to Philadelphia. He reported on his historic flight to President Washington. For, on this great day of January 9, 1793, Jean-Pierre Blanchard helped open a new American frontier. He showed us that we could not only *look* to the skies, we could soar up into them.

Jean-Pierre Blanchard
and Benjamin Franklin

JEAN-PIERRE FRANCOIS BLANCHARD (1753–1809) was born in Petit Andelys, France. As a boy, he invented all kinds of gadgets. His first experiments with flight began in the 1770s. His career — and life — took off when he began his work with balloons shortly after the first demonstrations by the Montgolfier brothers in 1783. He first flew in a balloon in March 1784 and he made his famous crossing of the English Channel in 1785. Blanchard also experimented with parachutes. Blanchard's balloon flight was actually not the first flight in the New World, but his was the most famous because of its association with President Washington. Edward Carnes of Maryland sent up a manned balloon in Philadelphia in 1784. Jean-Pierre died in 1809 after suffering a heart attack while flying in a balloon.

BENJAMIN FRANKLIN (1706–1790) was the American Ambassador to France during the first ballooning experiments by the Montgolfier brothers. Franklin was excited by what he saw. When a fellow spectator asked what this new invention could be used for, Franklin gave a response which is now famous, "What is the use of a new-born baby?" He knew this "new-born baby" — flight — had a great future!

Pirates!

ON NOVEMBER 5, 1798 an American ship, the *Pigou* [pee-shoo], set sail out of Philadelphia, headed for China for the tenth time in her maritime career. The *Pigou* was a good-sized but not a big ship, about 90 to 100 feet long. She weighed 360 tons, had a crew of 37 men, and carried TEN guns. (Ships are nearly always called "she"!)

In those days, merchant ships needed guns because the high seas were dangerous. England and France were at war and their warships might be anywhere on the Atlantic Ocean. Safe to say, the *Pigou* would not fare well if she got caught in the crossfire between two big warships.

But, even worse? Privateers! A privateer, not much different from a pirate ship, could seize a merchant ship like the *Pigou,* and keep any booty it captured. And, the *Pigou* had plenty of booty. Stowed aboard were lumber, lead, ginseng, iron, and lots and lots of dollars.

William Sansom of Philadelphia owned all this cargo. It was worth about $30,000, which today would be millions of dollars. He hoped to turn a handsome profit selling it in China. Then the *Pigou* would make the return journey, loaded with cargo from China which he could sell for another handsome profit in Philadelphia.

Buying and selling cargo in this global economy was the way William Sansom built his fortune. He was a smart businessman.

And as a smart businessman, he needed to protect his investment — *just in case!* So, he bought an insurance policy from Philadelphia's Insurance Company of North America, the first company of its kind in the new United States. He paid a total of $9,000 in premiums, plus $1.50 for a copy of the policy. *Just in case!*

So, well-loaded and well-insured, the *Pigou* began her journey.

Down the Delaware River, into the Chesapeake Bay, then out into the Atlantic she sailed. The sailors swabbed the decks, they raised and lowered sails, and they checked to see that the cargo was safe and sound. All was well as they headed for Bermuda.

Then, one chilly November night, the ship's master, John Green thought he saw something on the horizon . . . Actually, he thought he saw *two* somethings!

This was *not* good. The high seas were always dangerous . . .

but now, they were even more dangerous . . .

because French privateers often trolled these same waters . . .

right where the poor little *Pigou* was . . .

This very minute!

John Green yelled to his crew, "Man your battle stations!"

They did.

But . . . five minutes went by . . . ten minutes . . . half an hour. And . . . nothing!

So, he said, "Men, resume your positions."

The sailors did as they were told and returned to their chores . . .

But then, uh-oh!

Those two *somethings* Green thought he saw?

Those two *somethings* now had their sails up!

And they were heading right for the

Pigou!

And these were BIG *somethings!* Ships with FORTY-FOUR guns, and each with a crew of about 280 really big, beefy, sailors.

The poor little *Pigou's* puny little TEN guns were no match for these two huge frigates. And before they could say,

"Please don't shoot!"

✳ BAM! ✳ — Two cannon shots!

Right in the *Pigou's* stern!

Quickly the ship turned into a swirl of smoke, noise and lots of desperate sailors running around.

And then the worst happened. The ships were privateers and they seized the *Pigou!*

Those privateers took cash. They took the cargo — all $30,000 of it. They left the *Pigou* bare. And that's not all they stripped. They even took the sailors' clothes! Then, they kidnapped the naked crew, tossed them on their pirate ships, and off they sailed.

Loaded with all the stolen booty, one ship headed to Newfoundland. The other headed to the port of L'Orient in France where it landed on December 5. There the privateers threw ten of the *Pigou's* crew into prison . . . a dank, cold, dark prison . . . for no good reason!

This *could* be the end of the story . . . But, it's not, because back in Philadelphia, William Sansom was FURIOUS! He was rip-roaring mad!

His ship? Gone.

Cargo? Gone.

All his investments? Gone, gone, *gone!!!* That band of French privateer hoodlums had stolen *everything!*

This could have been a disaster, but for that one little piece of paper — the insurance policy which Mr. Sansom purchased — *Just in case!*

So, Mr. Sansom pulled out his copy of the policy, walked over to the Insurance Company of North America, showed it to them, and they reimbursed him for all his losses.

Furious Mr. Sansom was now happy.

But, how about the cold and naked crew sitting in the prison in France?

There was good news on that front too. The American Consul, Aaron Vasil sprang them from jail. No longer naked, out they walked, pleased as they could be, wearing some brand new clothes!

Historical Notes

Tʜᴇ Iɴsᴜʀᴀɴᴄᴇ Cᴏᴍᴘᴀɴʏ of North America opened for business in 1792, making it the oldest fire and marine insurance company in the United States. The account of the *Pigou* is part of its extensive archival collection.

A *privateer*, is a ship owned by an individual person or a group of people. It is armed at their expense. During times of war, a country can authorize a privateer to wage war out on the high seas. If a privateer captures an enemy ship — or a ship believed to be an enemy ship — it can keep much of the cargo on that captured ship. The word *privateers* is used to describe the crew on a privateer ship. Privateers would rather be called that than . . . pirates!

The Sailor and Isaac Hopper: Inventors of the Underground Railroad?

THE UNDERGROUND RAILROAD is famous. So are some of its most famous conductors, people like Harriet Tubman and Sojourner Truth. They, and so many others, dedicated their lives to helping slaves win freedom by traveling from the South to the North, even as far as Canada. But how did the Underground Railroad get its start?

Many believe it began in Philadelphia, long before the Civil War, way back in the 1780s and 1790s. One of its earliest leaders was Isaac Hopper who lived in Philadelphia.

It all started when Isaac was just sixteen years old. That's when Isaac moved from his farm in New Jersey to Philadelphia, the biggest city in the new United States. It was 1787. So much was happening up at the Pennsylvania State House, now called Independence Hall. Delegates from each of the new United States were meeting, and talking, and arguing — all through a long, hot summer. They were writing the new Constitution for the new United States. Everyone was talking about . . .

Liberty! Freedom! Independence!

Such thrilling words and inspiring ideas which we cherish as Americans.

But even as Isaac Hopper heard these words he must have thought about an elderly man he had known since childhood. Mingo.

Mingo worked on a farm in New Jersey. With deep emotion, he told Isaac stories. Stories about his homeland, Africa. About how he was captured by slave catchers when he was a child back in Africa. And how he was brought to America — enslaved.

Mingo and his story made a deep impression on young Isaac. For, not long after arriving in Philadelphia, he did what can only be described as an amazing thing. . . . Let's go back and watch history unfold. . . .

The year is 1787. Isaac Hopper is sixteen years old and he's standing on the edge of the Delaware River. The wind blows through his shaggy black hair and turns his pale cheeks pink.

He watches as ships bob up and down in the water. He looks up at their tall masts and the piers piled high with barrels and cargo.

Suddenly, he sees something. Someone is hiding, there in the shadows! A sailor!

Quietly, Isaac moves toward him.

Quietly, the dark-skinned sailor edges closer and tells Isaac his story. He is enslaved. He has escaped his ship. He wants to be free. But, he is a fugitive, and he needs help.

Isaac whispers oh so quietly, so nobody but the sailor can hear,

> "I know someone who might be able to help. Hide
> here behind these barrels tonight. Tomorrow
> night I will bring a letter of introduction and some
> directions to the house of a person who will help
> you hide from your owner."

The sailor nods, then just as quietly, whispers,

> "That's a good plan, but what happens next?"

And they continue:

> "Hmmmmm. . . . Let's see. I'll ask that friend to
> find another hiding place for you if you need to keep
> moving farther from your owner."

"Good plan. But what if someone comes looking for me or if I need to keep moving? What if one of these "friends" . . . betrays me?"

"Well, we'll have to find friends we can trust completely and who will help you hide or travel farther still if there is danger."

"Sounds like we have a plan."

Such a simple plan! And, such a plan filled with so many risks!

To do it, Isaac and the sailor had to trust each other with their lives, even though they had just met. How many people are willing to do that?

Then, it meant trusting lots of other people, all those friends of friends.

Even riskier? What happened if a slave catcher heard about this sailor and went and found him in his hiding place?

Simple. The sailor would be returned to his master. And punished. And once again enslaved.

And what about Isaac and all of his friends? If they were caught, they could be fined, or humiliated, or even put in prison.

Those were the risks. *Real* risks, most especially for the sailor.

But, what if the plan worked?

Simple. The sailor would be free!

Here is the amazing thing. This simple yet bold plan worked! With each day that he hid and with each friend who helped, the sailor got closer and closer to freedom. Then, after six months and one day, the rules of Pennsylvania law declared that the sailor was . . .

A free man!

With freedom, this sailor started a whole new life — on the land — as a farmer. A *free* farmer.

The sailor's successful journey set the example for others seeking new lives as free men, women and children, which makes him one of the inventors of the Underground Railroad.

And Isaac?

That one night along the Delaware River set the course for the rest of his life. He learned that with imagination and ingenuity he could assist others who, like the sailor, wished to be free. So, one by one, night by night, and friend by friend, Isaac Hopper formed a network of people who helped men, women and children escape slavery and achieve freedom. One by one, night by night, and friend by friend, this daring, law-defying system came to be called the Underground Railroad.

Isaac Hopper

ISAAC TATUM HOPPER (1771–1852) was born in New Jersey, moved to Philadelphia in 1787 and remained there until 1829 when he left for New York City. As a young man, Isaac joined the Society of Friends, or Quakers as most people still call them. Quakers were among the most active leaders in the abolition movement. Isaac trained as a tailor but schooled himself at law which he used to great advantage to help people win freedom. He knew the laws so well that over forty years he likely helped as many as 1000 people win their freedom. Hopper supported schools for children and adult freed persons, and he worked for prison reform. Many people found his beliefs too extreme. But others, both white and black, admired and loved him. A fugitive woman once said, "I would trust that Quaker gentleman anywhere. Let us go with him."

Doctor Mom

WHAT DO YOU DO when you wake up and feel . . . *agghhh* . . . awful!

You take some aspirin! You call the doctor! Or, you call . . . *"Mom!!!"*

What did people do 200 years ago when they woke up and felt . . . *aggghhh* . . . awful?

They did pretty much the same thing. They took some medicine. They called the doctor. Or, they called . . . *"Mom!!!"*

But medicine was just a little different back then. In fact, medicine could be a pretty risky business — especially if you went to the doctor.

Back then, doctors trained in England or Scotland, then starting in 1765, they could go to medical school in Philadelphia at what is now the University of Pennsylvania.

If you had a cough, if you had a fever, if you had some other illness, doctors worked to cure you.

If you said,

"I feel weak!"

The doctor put creepy, crawly leeches on your arms to suck out all the bad blood in your veins!

If you said,

"My heart feels funny!"

leeches

The doctor said,

"Here's some . . . foxglove!"

If you said,

"My tooth hurts!"

foxglove

The doctor said,

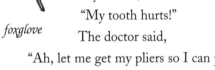

"Ah, let me get my pliers so I can pull that bad tooth out!"

At the drop of his tricorn hat, the doctor might say, let's try mercury! Or lead! Or iron filings! Or, how about some . . . whale oil!

The fact is, some of these treatments worked. For example, foxglove, a plant which is also called digitalis, is still used by doctors to treat heart conditions.

But a whole lot of these cures didn't work, which meant that doctors often made patients sicker, and sometimes they even died — of the cure! Doctors tried, but science was very limited back then.

But, what if you were just kinda sick, not so sick that you needed a doctor. What if you just felt . . . kinda lousy?

Back then, just like today, women were often the ones who took care of everyday illnesses in the family. Back then, though, moms couldn't run to the drug store and buy aspirin or cough syrup. Instead, moms made their own medicines, moms like Hannah Haines, for example. Hannah lived in Philadelphia with her family, and she kept a recipe book where she wrote down all the medicines she made for them.

Hannah's first patient? Her first child, Reuben, born in 1786. Oh, poor Reuben! He had terrible colic, which meant that he cried and screamed a lot. Things got desperate, so Hannah mixed up this potion:

A Cure for Cholick

Take the rinds of four fresh China Oranges, four pints of good Spirits of Brandy, twelve or fifteen Cloves, two Nutmegs, grated fine, a quarter of a Pound of Raisins, one teaspoonful of aniseed, mix and steep the above two days, shaking it the first when made and after settling, it is fit for use. Take a table-spoonful with a little water. If that does not ease repeat it again.

brandy

It does have helpful ingredients such as the aniseed — licorice — which soothes upset stomachs. That, plus the orange juice, nutmeg and cloves meant that Hannah's potion also tasted good.

But what do you think the secret ingredient was in Hannah's Cure? Perhaps, those four pints of Brandy?

Two hundred years ago, all kinds of remedies and cures included various forms of strong beverages — even for children and little babies like Reuben. We don't do that today.

Hannah had lots of other potions besides her Cure for Cholick. She had a cure for . . . worms! Next time you have that problem, try her "Corrosive sublimate of Mercury" mixed with more of that brandy.

If you survived all these cures and made it to old age, Hannah might have mixed up a special treat, with extra nutritional qualities guaranteed to help the aged feel young again. Here is her special recipe.

eels

A Youth Tonic

Take six small eels washed clean & skin stript off . . . cut them, put them into a pint of water with a little salt. . . . add two blades of mace, six whole peppercorns, and a little parsley, then let them stew about half an hour; and the broth will be fit for use.

Mmmmm. Yummy eels. Thanks Doctor Mom!

Now don't try any of this at home, but when you do get home, do say thank you to your doctor and your mom for all their good medical care.

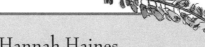

Hannah Haines

HANNAH MARSHALL HAINES (1765–1828) lived in Philadelphia and nearby Germantown all her life. She married Caspar Wistar Haines in 1785 and their son Reuben was born the next year. Caspar's parents died during the terrible Yellow Fever epidemic which killed about one-tenth of Philadelphia's population in 1793. To escape the Fever, the young family fled to the relative safety of their country house, Wyck, which still stands in Germantown. Hannah wrote many letters, kept diaries, and assembled recipe books during her long life. They survive and are now part of the Wyck Papers housed at the American Philosophical Society. Hannah's son Reuben (1786–1831) survived his colic and his mother's cures which is a good thing because he became a leader in Philadelphia, helping found the Academy of Natural Sciences, the Franklin Institute, and the Pennsylvania Horticultural Society.

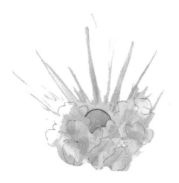

Cross that Line!
Harriet Tubman and the
Underground Railroad

EVER HEAR of a woman named Araminta Ross? She was born in 1822 in Maryland. Some called her Minty. Minty Ross. Ring any bells?

What if you knew that Minty changed her name, then later changed her life, then later still, helped change the lives of many people?

Ever hear of Harriet Tubman? Well, that was Minty, one of the most amazing heroes of the Underground Railroad. When she was a young woman, Minty changed her name to Harriet, which was her mother's name. At about the same time she married a man named John Tubman, so everyone came to know her as Harriet Tubman.

Harriet's freedom journey began back in 1849 when she was 27 years old.

She had lived in Maryland her whole life, enslaved. When she was just a girl, she suffered cruel whippings, and once, an overseer hit her so hard with a lead weight that it knocked her unconscious. This left her with powerful headaches until the day she died. But, it also gave her a powerful mission, and a remarkable ability to see the invisible, sometimes in the dark of night and sometimes in her dreams.

Harriet's powerful mission drove her. She wanted freedom. Freedom for herself. Freedom for her family. Freedom for others who lived in slavery. And her ability to see the invisible and move in the dark? Well, it came in handy, at least fourteen times, to be exact.

But all this gets ahead of the story, because back in 1849 Harriet was in a fix. She had tried escaping her master once before. The first time? It was with her two brothers.

As brothers and sisters sometimes do, they argued about which path to take, "This one!" said one, "That one!" said the other. Going nowhere fast, the brothers lost their nerve and all three turned around, walking back to slavery.

From that, Harriet knew she had to try again, especially after she heard rumors that her master might sell her and send her south. The Deep South! Far from her home, her family, and her husband.

Those rumors got Harriet thinking. She knew that to be free, she had to leave Maryland.

This time, though, she decided to make the journey alone, without her brothers, even without her husband. All alone, she prepared herself to leave behind everything she knew.

So, one dark night, Harriet began her journey.

Imagine her.

Frightened.

Determined.

Alone.

The wind is blowing. She looks up. There are a few stars . . . She looks for the North Star, pointing in the direction she needs to travel. She sings a song to boost her spirits.

"Hail oh hail, ye happy spirits,

Death no more shall make you fear."

Sounds easy enough, doesn't it? Just follow a star, sing a song? Right?

Wrong. Harriet well remembered how she and her brothers failed in their first attempt, and she knew that escaping from Maryland — alone — and traveling 100 miles on foot in the dark — alone — all to reach Pennsylvania — a free state — this was hard! No question she had plenty of courage. But she needed more help than just a star shining up there, far, far away in the sky.

What would happen, she wondered, if it was cloudy and there were no stars out?

What would happen, she wondered, if there were two paths in front of her, not just one?

What would happen, she wondered, if she was caught?

Harriet knew the answer to that.

All those questions meant that Harriet needed a plan and she needed some help.

Help came from a woman in Maryland who agreed to shelter Harriet as she began the first leg of her journey. The plan grew from that.

This woman knew another woman farther along who could also help. And that woman? She knew another person who could do the same thing.

And so it went, for Harriet was now making her journey from station master to station master on the Underground Railroad. Closer and closer she got to Pennsylvania. A free state. And freedom. Her freedom.

At last she arrived at the boundary line separating Delaware — a slave state — and Pennsylvania — a free state.

That line is invisible to the eye, but remember, Harriet could see the invisible. So, she took a step, a step she never forgot. Years later she remembered that astonishing moment.

> "When I found I had crossed that line, I looked at my hands to see if I was the same person. There was such glory over everything; the sun came like gold through the trees and over the fields, and I felt like I was in Heaven. I had crossed the line."

One hundred miles on foot, in wagons, at night, then — with one step — Harriet Tubman was a free woman!

For most people, the story could end there, but not for Harriet. She settled in Philadelphia for a spell. Here she was surrounded by a lively community that was completely new to her. Here were people of color who were free! They ran businesses, they went to school, they had their own churches, they helped others in need, especially fugitives from slavery just like Harriet.

Harriet settled happily in to this free black community of Philadelphia. She worked hard, she saved some money . . . but then she got restless. Others wanted to be free, just like her. Simple and pure, she heard a call.

> "The lord who told me to take care of my people meant me to do it just so long as I live, and so I do what he told me to do."

So, to take care of her people, Harriet left the safety of free Philadelphia and headed south for the slave state of Maryland so she could help others make the journey to freedom.

She did this over and over, at least thirteen times, back and forth. She helped her parents, her brothers, and her friends,

Cross that line!

Each time she went, she risked her own freedom. Yet still she went, so others could

Cross that line!

The journey was oh so long, and oh so hard, stretching as it did from Maryland all the way to Canada, the safest place for a fugitive to start a new life. But with Harriet leading the way, seventy people, and maybe more

Cross that line!

Sometimes they were tired, sometimes they were afraid. One frightened man pleaded to stop and rest. But with slave catchers on their tail, Harriet held a pistol to his head: "Move or die." He moved, and followed Harriet all the way to Canada and freedom.

Over the course of a long life, she was called Minty Ross . . . Harriet Tubman . . . General Tubman . . . The Moses of her People . . . What's your favorite?

Now, shout it out!

Then, let's all remember the woman who helped so many

Cross that line!

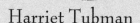

Harriet Tubman

HARRIET TUBMAN (1822–1913) was born a slave in Maryland and died a free woman at her home in Auburn, New York. Besides her work with the Underground Railroad, she served as a spy for the Union army during the Civil War, she nursed Union soldiers and freed men and women, and she supported women's suffrage. Though illiterate, she founded schools for freed black children in the South. She also founded the Harriet Tubman Home for Indigent Aged Negroes in New York. She had many admirers. The radical abolitionist John Brown called her General Tubman, the writer Sarah Bradford called her The Moses of Her People in 1869, and in 1868 Frederick Douglass wrote her and said, "Excepting John Brown — of sacred memory — I know of no one who has willingly encountered more perils and hardships to serve our enslaved people than you have."

NOTE: There is a long-held tradition that Harriet made a total of nineteen trips to Maryland which helped bring 300 people to freedom. Historians now believe that Harriet Tubman made a total of fourteen trips from Maryland to Pennsylvania, the first trip being her own journey to freedom. On the other thirteen she helped at least seventy enslaved African-Americans make their own journeys to freedom, and indirectly enabled about fifty others to make their own escapes.

It Be Me, Peter

Amazing grace! How sweet the sound
That saved a wretch like me!
I once was lost, but now am found;
Was blind, but now I see.

This true story could easily be called "Amazing Grace," for it is about lost brothers who found each other in the most amazing way. The story begins in 1807 on a plantation in Maryland.

Sidney, an enslaved woman, yearned to be free. Her husband, Levin, had purchased his freedom and now lived in New Jersey. She wanted to join him — as a free woman. She tried to escape once, bringing her four children with her. A slave catcher found them and returned them all to their plantation and enslavement.

Now Sidney faced a truly awful decision. Her desire for

freedom was so strong, but she knew she could never succeed if she traveled with all four children. She decided to risk taking her two young daughters with her, leaving behind her two older sons in the care of their grandmother. Maybe then, she could reach her husband and freedom. And then, maybe, they could find a way to win freedom for their sons.

When the time came, Sidney kissed the head of six-year old Peter, knowing she might never see him again. Tears streamed down the cheeks of the scared little boy.

The next morning "Master" discovered that Sidney and her daughters had escaped! In furious retaliation, he sold Peter and his brother Levin. Over the next forty years different "Masters" sold them time and again, taking the brothers from

Maryland's Eastern shore, to Kentucky, and at last to the brutal cotton plantations of Alabama. With each sale, the brothers moved farther from their parents, and farther from freedom.

Though enslaved, Peter resisted the conditions of his life with every ounce of his strength and he kept alive his dream of freedom.

Then, one awful night, men carried his brother Levin back to the slave quarters. He had been badly beaten with 317 lashes of the whip for attempting to visit his wife at a neighboring plantation. Levin died and Peter buried his brother. He vowed he would not die enslaved.

Peter considered his options — there were only two. He could attempt escape like his mother, or, he could purchase his freedom like his father. In the end he chose his father's path. To do this Peter first persuaded Joseph Friedman, a sympathetic white merchant, to purchase him from his "Master." When not working for Friedman, Peter hired himself out to earn the money he needed — $500. At last, he had *just* enough money! What he didn't have, was the additional money needed to purchase freedom for his wife and three children. So, like his mother, Peter faced an awful decision, and he knew he would have to follow her example in his quest. He left his wife and children, vowing he would win their freedom after he had won his own.

Peter began his journey north from Alabama accompanied by Joseph's brother, Isaac. At last they reached Ohio, a free state! Isaac Friedman signed the necessary papers which set Peter free, and Peter continued his journey. He remembered his family lived somewhere near the Delaware River. He wondered,

> "Do they still live there? Who is still alive? Did my Momma and Poppa have more children, brothers and sisters who don't even know me?"

With hope, Peter headed east and made the long trip from Ohio to Pennsylvania. At last he arrived in Philadelphia, on the Delaware River.

Peter felt lost and bewildered in the big, bustling city. How could he find his loved ones? He inquired at black churches throughout the city. No one could help him. Finally, he met a minister, Reverend Byas, who took him to the Pennsylvania Anti-Slavery Society.

On August 1, 1850, Peter entered the Society's office, hoping to gain some clue about his family. There, seated at a desk, was a man whose face was as black as his own. He was the Secretary for the Pennsylvania Anti-Slavery Society and he carefully recorded the names and stories of fugitives who arrived in Philadelphia. He looked up.

> "Your name?" he asked.

> "Peter. Peter Friedman."

Then Peter began to tell his story. As each detail unfolded — his mother's escape, so long ago, her name ("*Sidney*"), the name of his father ("*Levin*"), all of this was familiar to the Secretary. In amazement he looked at Peter.

> "My feelings were unutterable. I could see in the face of my new found brother, the likeness of my mother."

William Still, Secretary to the Pennsylvania Anti-Slavery Society, was meeting his older brother Peter for the first time! He looked at Peter and said,

> "Suppose I should tell you that I am your brother?"

Imagine the astonishment and joy these two brothers felt with this amazing discovery!

William then told his brother that though their father had died, their mother still lived just across the Delaware River. On August 3, Peter traveled with William, his sister Kitturah and two other newly found siblings to the Pine Barrens of New Jersey. They went to their mother's house, something Peter had dreamed about but thought might never happen. He had not seen her since she kissed him good bye when he was six years old. He went inside, and there she was.

Tears streamed down Peter's face. "Momma! It be me, Peter!"

His mother, now old and fragile, held him tight just as she had so long ago.

Finally, she asked, "Where is your brother, Levin?"

He paused. How could he tell her that Levin was dead?

"He be free, Momma."

She lifted her eyes to heaven and cried, "Thank God Almighty!"

Her two babies were free.

> *Through many dangers, toils and snares*
> *I have already come;*
> *'Tis Grace that brought me safe thus far*
> *and Grace will lead me home.*

Peter Still

PETER (1801–1868), son of Sidney and Levin, took the name Friedman when he began his freedom journey in 1850. He subsequently changed it to Freedman, then, in 1854 he changed it to Still, the name of his family. Peter Still's quest for freedom did not end in 1850. He needed to free his wife and children, and bring them north so that they could live together as a family. To meet their purchase price of $5000, Peter went on a speaking tour where he described his personal experiences. By 1854 he collected the required sum, and he brought his reunited and now free family to New Jersey where they lived on a farm near other members of his family. Peter's brother William Still (1821–1902) was one of the most famous leaders of the Underground Railroad. He later published a massive record of the activities that revolved around his office at the Pennsylvania Anti-Slavery Society. His *Underground Rail Road: Authentic Narratives and First-Hand Accounts* (1872) remains the single most important document of this extraordinary chapter in America's quest for freedom and liberty for all its citizens.

Thirty-Four Stars: Abraham Lincoln Visits Independence Hall

IN FEBRUARY 1861, Abraham Lincoln traveled by train from his home in Illinois to Washington, D.C. where he would soon be inaugurated as the sixteenth President of the United States. As part of the journey, he stopped in Philadelphia so that he could make a speech in front of Independence Hall.

Excited crowds awaited his arrival in Philadelphia on the evening of February 21. Some came to honor their new leader. Others came to jeer at the man whose stand on slavery had stirred rebellion in the Southern states. As throngs cheered and jeered, fireworks exploded and sparklers gleamed with the words . . .

Abraham Lincoln!
The Whole Union!

The next morning, Philadelphians eagerly prepared for the celebration. One Philadelphian, Charles Alexander, later wrote about this unforgettable day.

He remembered how nervous he had been as he put on his finest clothes. It was a very cold day, he recalled, so he bundled up before walking over to Independence Hall. Patriotic bunting hung from many buildings, and everywhere Charles looked there were people — on the streets, even on the roofs. Everyone hoped to catch a glimpse of the ceremonies.

As a city dignitary, Charles had a special invitation for a reception inside the east room of Independence Hall, the same room where the nation had been born. He entered and there he saw Abraham Lincoln standing in front of a statue of George Washington. One by one, leading Philadelphians approached him. Charles got closer and closer, and then at last, it was his turn to greet the President-elect. Lincoln reached out to shake his hand. How big it was! Charles's hand nearly got lost in its grasp. No wonder many called Lincoln The Railsplitter, for this was a strong hand that had done hard work.

Soon after, Charles and the other guests left the building to sit on a platform just outside Independence Hall. Thousands of ordinary Philadelphians stood out in the cold and waited to hear Lincoln's words. At last the tall man rose and spoke.

> *"I am filled with deep emotion at finding myself standing here in the place where were collected together the wisdom, the patriotism, the devotion to principle, from which sprung the institutions under which we live."*

Lincoln continued, despite many interruptions by the cheering and applauding crowd.

> *"I have often inquired of myself, what great principle or idea it was that kept this Confederacy so long together. It was not the mere matter of the separation of the colonies from the mother land; but something in that Declaration giving liberty, not alone to the people of this country, but hope to the world for all future time."*

When he finished his inspiring words, Lincoln turned to the final piece of the ceremonies. It was time to raise a brand new flag on the flag pole of Independence Hall. This new flag had thirty-four stars including its newest star representing the state of Kansas, just admitted to the Union. Some had wanted Kansas to be a slave state, making slavery legal. Others wanted it to be a free state. After years of violent confrontations between the two groups, Kansas was now a state, a *free* state in the United States.

Lincoln stepped up to the flag pole and took the rope. The cold February wind picked up. He took off his overcoat and reached for the line. With both hands he began to pull. With each stroke the new flag began to rise . . .

> higher,
>> higher,
>>> then suddenly . . .

The flag snagged on the roof!

Everyone gasped. But then, The Railsplitter spat on both hands, and reached for another pull. With three hearty tugs, the flag reached the top!

Cheers rang out and the band struck up a popular tune, *The Star Spangled Banner.* Newspaper stories described the memorable day and drawings captured the dramatic moment when the President-elect personally raised the new flag so it could fly proudly above the nation's birthplace.

Still, as Charles Alexander and thousands of other Philadelphians left the ceremonies, they must have wondered — What *was* the future of this Union with its thirty-four states?

As he headed to Washington and his inauguration, Lincoln wondered the same.

The answer came less than two months later. On April 12, 1861, the army of the new Confederate States of America fired its guns upon Fort Sumter in South Carolina, marking the start of the Civil War. Thirty-four hours later, on April 14, Major Robert Anderson of the United States Army surrendered the fort. The American flag with its thirty-four stars

came down the flag pole to be replaced by the Confederate flag.

Exactly four years later, Union troops recaptured the Fort. On April 14, 1865, Major Robert Anderson raised the *same* thirty-four star flag which had come down in 1861. The bloody Civil War was over. The Union was again whole. The United States was reunited.

Abraham Lincoln and Philadelphia

PHILADELPHIA and the documents written here — the Declaration of Independence and the Constitution — inspired much of Lincoln's thinking and writing. He knew that the country was in deep crisis when he visited in February 1861, so he used his speech at Independence Hall to remind Americans of the words and deeds which created the nation. His Gettysburg Address, written in November 1863, echoed key phrases in both documents. Lincoln was fatally shot on April 14, 1865, the same day that Union troops recaptured Fort Sumter, and one week after Confederate General Robert E. Lee surrendered to Union General Ulysses S. Grant. Americans mourned as Lincoln's funeral train traveled slowly from Washington to Illinois. On the way, Lincoln's body lay in state in Independence Hall. Thousands waited in line for hours to pay their respects to the man who gave his life to preserve the Union.

The Vexillologist.

HAVE YOU EVER run across the word *vexillologist?*

Here are some clues about what it means.

What do you call a person who digs in the earth to discover clues about the past?

An archaeo — *logist!*

What do you call a person who studies nature and natural resources?

An eco — *logist!*

And, finally, what do you call someone who studies animals?

A zoo — *logist!*

So a vexil — *lologist* studies . . .

Vexills???

Here's another clue. A vexillologist would be *very* interested in Betsy Ross and what she made.

Because . . . a vexillologist studies flags! . . . And Betsy Ross sewed a *lot* of flags starting in about 1776.

Betsy Ross was an upholsterer who lived in Philadelphia. Before the Revolutionary War, she sewed slipcovers for chairs and ruffles for shirts. But during the war, she used her needle to sew flags for the Pennsylvania Navy. While those new flags flapped on ship masts, the United States Congress passed a resolution on June 14, 1777.

Resolved: that the flag of the United States be made of thirteen Stripes, alternate red and white; that the Union be thirteen Stars, white in a blue field, representing a new Constellation.

Lots of people believe that Betsy Ross sewed flags that fit that description, with thirteen alternating red and white stripes and thirteen stars arranged in a circle — a Constellation — on a blue field.

Over the years, Betsy Ross has had many fans. But one of her biggest admirers?

. . . A *vexillologist* named Charles Weisgerber!

Charles was a young and hungry artist living in Philadelphia back in 1892. One day he read about a contest. The City of Philadelphia would award a prize of $1000 to the person who painted the best picture of a local historical event. This was a huge sum of money, plus the winning picture would hang at the Chicago World's Fair in 1893 where *millions* of people would see it.

Hmmm, Charles thought. "I sure could use $1000! I wonder what I could paint?"

Charles picked up his paintbrushes and began walking around Philadelphia, a great place to find historical subjects. Independence Hall, the Liberty Bell, Ben Franklin, those were easy. TOO easy for Charles. He needed something different, something nobody else had thought of, something *so* good it would win that big prize.

One day he stumbled upon a little place called Mund's Tavern located at 239 Arch Street.

Charles sat down and started talking to the tavern owner. He said something like this,

> "There's this contest . . . I need an idea. . . . I want to win!"

The tavern keeper looked at Charles with sympathy, then said something rather like,

> "Sir, have you come to the right place! Did you
> know that this very tavern was once the home of
> Betsy Ross? And Betsy Ross is the woman who
> SEWED THE FIRST AMERICAN FLAG?!"

Charles perked up.

> "Betsy Ross!!! . . . Where have I heard that name
> before?"

Betsy Ross was not *exactly* a household name in 1892. But
Charles had heard of her because in 1871 Betsy's grandson
wrote a paper and gave a speech about his grandmother's stories. As an old woman, Betsy told her family about the flags
she sewed during the Revolution. She described a visit to her
house by her uncle George Ross, Robert Morris and George
Washington. She said they asked her to sew a flag with
stars — *six*-pointed stars. According to Betsy, she replied, "a
five-pointed star would be easier!" Then she showed them
how to do it, by folding a piece of paper, *just* so, then snipping
it, *just* so. When she unfolded it, she held a perfect *five*-
pointed star. *Just* like the five-pointed stars on every American
flag since then.

"Betsy Ross," Charles thought. "That's my girl!"

Now that he had his subject, Charles Weisgerber began
his masterpiece. On an enormous canvas — nine feet high by

twelve feet across — he painted *The Birth of Our Nation's Flag*. Its stars? George Ross, Robert Morris, George Washington, and . . . Betsy Ross . . . with a thirteen-star flag draped over her lap. It was spectacular!

But, Charles *did* take a little artistic license in creating his masterpiece. After all, Betsy had died years before, so he couldn't ask her to pose. Plus, he didn't know what she looked like because she never had her portrait painted. Rather than see this as a problem, Charles imagined what she *might* have looked like.

> "Blue eyes, brown hair . . . hmmmm, that looks good."

Then there was another problem. Betsy never said she actually sat with those famous men and showed them her *finished* flag. Which means Charles made up an event and created a painting around it.

Still, his artistic license paid off, because Charles Weisgerber won the contest! He won the thousand-dollar prize, his painting got hung in the Pennsylvania Pavilion in Chicago, and he became a *vexillologist*. He loved flags so much, he even named his son. . . . Vexil Domus Weisgerber, Latin for "Flag House Weisgerber."

Charles also loved the place where his idea for the painting was born — Mund's Tavern. He organized a drive to save it and he asked American children to each contribute one dime to make sure that Mund's Tavern could become. . . The Betsy Ross House.

Those dimes added up and now visitors love seeing the house and hearing Betsy's story.

. . . And all of this because of a contest

and a painting

and that *Vexillologist!*

Betsy Ross and Charles Weisgerber

ELIZABETH GRISCOM ROSS ASHBURN CLAYPOOLE (1752–1836) was born into a large Quaker family in New Jersey. When she was three, her family moved to Philadelphia. Betsy attended school then apprenticed with John Webster, a well-known upholsterer. This training made Betsy somewhat unusual for most women of her day. Before the Revolutionary War she worked in the upholstery business, but once she started making flags she continued making them for over fifty years. Widowed twice, she married three times. She also made musket balls during the Revolution which made her a "Fighting Quaker" and a member of the Society of Free Quakers.

WHEN CHARLES WEISGERBER started his nation-wide campaign to save the Betsy Ross House, he sent each contributor a small, 10-color print of his painting called a chromolithograph. One dime at a time, he raised the $25,000 he needed to buy the house, refurbish it and make it into a museum. The Betsy Ross House welcomes thousands of visitors each year to learn more about the seamstress who snipped those stars, "*just so!*"

The Birth of Television: The Philo T. Farnsworth Story

BEN FRANKLIN. Thomas Edison. George Washington Carver. What do they have in common?

They were inventors! They invented all kinds of things. Bifocals! (That's Franklin). Light bulbs and phonographs! (That's Edison). Three hundred ways to use peanuts, including using it as fuel for cars! (That's George Washington Carver).

Now, try this. Philo T. Farnsworth!

Ever hear of him?

These clues might help.

What is something that — teaches the alphabet?

What is something that allows you to watch your home team — even if you aren't sitting in the stadium or ballpark?

What's something we so take for granted — that we often tune it out?

Figured it out?
Of course! It's TV!
And Philo T. Farnsworth? He's the guy who invented it, and he started when he was just fourteen years old. That's when he was living with his family on a farm in Idaho.

Everybody called Philo *Phil,* so imagine Phil back on his farm, plowing a potato field. Back and forth, row after row. Most people would look at those rows and say,

"My, what lovely straight lines!"

Not Phil. He looked at those rows and said,

"Electronic television!"

Phil obviously was not your average kid, and when he looked at those rows, and said what he said, it was 1921 — and there was no such thing as "electronic television!" Back then, *radio* was a new invention. Movies were new too, but they were *silent* movies with no sound. In silent pictures, actors went through the motions of say, robbing a bank, but they could only mouth the words because there was no sound. Instead, Phil and his friends in the audience read the dialogue which flashed up onto the screen *after* the bank got robbed.

Phil liked *listening* to the radio and he liked *watching* silent movies. But even more, he *loved* playing with electricity.

He would think and tinker, tinker and think. Then one day he had a great idea . . .

> "Hmmmmm, maybe I can somehow combine radio with movies, and make a talking movie. Even better, maybe I can figure out how to send this talking movie RIGHT into somebody's home!"

Phil was *so* excited about his idea that he continued to work on it. On his last day of school in the spring of 1922, he shared his ideas with his science teacher, Justin Tolman. Mr. Tolman listened as Phil explained. . . .

> "I've got this idea. I've got to tell you about it because you're the only person I know who might understand it."

Phil pointed to the diagrams he had sketched onto the blackboard.

> "This is my idea for electronic television."

Mr. Tolman scratched his head and said,

> "Television? What's that?"

135

Phil wrote more formulas on the blackboard and continued, saying something rather like this. . . .

> "This is how to do it. You gotta capture light in a
> jar. Then you gotta transmit the light in a series
> of individual lines — rows and rows of individual
> electronic beams. They are like, well, like the rows
> and rows of potatoes I just planted at my dad's farm!"

Mr. Tolman scratched his head again and said, "Rows of potatoes??"

Phil continued.

> "Then you gotta deflect each line, magnetically, one
> at a time, then fit them all together to create — ta
> da! — a moving picture!"

Got that? Well, if you didn't, Mr. Tolman didn't quite get it either. Or, at least at first.

But Phil kept explaining, and at some point Mr. Tolman realized that this crazy idea just might work. He even tucked one of Phil's drawings into his pocket, a drawing that later proved that Phil invented TV — in 1922, when he was just fifteen years old.

Phil was sure his idea could work, so he kept thinking and tinkering, even while he was at college. That's where he learned useful information about radio, and vacuum tubes, and cathode ray tubes — not to zap space aliens — but to go inside his electronic television. He even built a television laboratory in San Francisco where he invented his Image Dissector. According to his plan, the Image Dissector would transmit an electronic image from his lab into another room where he had set up a receiver. But, would it work?

To find out, he set everything into motion. Suddenly, he heard a shout from his wife who was in the other room . . .

"I see a moving line on the receiver!"

Modest Phil announced,

"There you are, electronic television."

Electronic television. That was what Phil patented on January 7, 1927, which made him the Official Father of TV at the ripe old age of twenty-one.

But Phil still had one big problem. He had figured out the *idea* of television. He just hadn't quite figured out how to make it *work* in a way that would make it available to lots of people.

He kept at it, and eventually landed in Philadelphia where he worked for Philco, a company which made radios. In his lab he thought and tinkered and experimented. So did other inventors who had their own ideas about TV. The race was on, but at last Phil *had* it, and he was ready to show the world.

So, on a summer day in 1934, Phil and Philadelphia invited the public to the Franklin Institute, named for another great inventor. Thousands of Philadelphians lined up to enter the building. As they did, they walked past a camera. They walked a little farther, then surprise! Suddenly, they saw themselves on a "receiver" — which was nothing more than the bottom of a ten gallon jug.

The guests smiled and waved at themselves on that ten gallon jug receiver. They LOVED it.

After they finished waving to themselves, the guests entered a room to watch specially produced shows — on Phil's TV! Athletes, singers, dancers, politicians! Sound familiar?

The audience went wild. They LOVED TV! They WANTED TV!

It took more time to perfect television, but by the 1950s millions of Americans watched TV shows in their own homes, just as Phil had imagined back on his farm in Idaho.

So, next time you watch your favorite show? Remember it was brought to you by — Philo T. Farnsworth, the Father of TV.

Philo T. Farnsworth

PHILO TAYLOR FARNSWORTH (1906–1971) was born in Utah in a log cabin. He and his five brothers and sisters moved with the parents from Utah to Idaho when he was eleven, traveling in three covered wagons. Upon arriving to their new farm in Idaho, Phil discovered a treasure trove of magazines stashed up in the attic including *Popular Science* and *Science and Invention.* These introduced him to the inventions of Thomas Edison, Alexander Graham Bell, and Albert Einstein. Phil read avidly, and he also became the family's resident electrician before he started high school at the age of fourteen. Though Phil never graduated from high school or college, he became one of the most important inventors of the twentieth century.

Smart Cookies

WHO DOESN'T LOVE a good cookie?

Mmmmm. Chocolate chip. Oatmeal. Sugar. Ginger snaps. All are so delicious it can be hard to choose a favorite.

And, for cookie lovers, what is the favorite time of year?

Easy! Girl Scout Cookie Time!

It's a time to satisfy that cookie hunger while also supporting a very good cause. That's why *lots* of us buy *lots* of cookies from *lots* of young women wearing Girl Scout uniforms. They sell all those cookies to support the activities for which Girl Scouts are famous — hiking, camping, trips, helping out in communities, building leadership and pride. They also sell all those cookies because . . . We love them!

Not many people know that Girl Scout cookies and Philadelphia share a little bit of history, but here's the delicious story.

The Girl Scouts of the USA got their start back in 1912, two years after the Boy Scouts of America had begun. The Boy Scouts were out there hiking, and fishing, and camping, and a sassy young lady thought,

"Girls can do that, too!"

So Juliette "Daisy" Lowe decided to organize the first Girl Scout meeting in America in Savannah, Georgia, her hometown. Her troop began with 18 members who wanted to be smart, strong and awesome, just like Daisy. Quicker than you can say the Girl Scout Pledge, the Girl Scouts took off because girls all over the country loved hiking, camping, and building leadership together. Today, there are more than three million members.

The problem was that all these great Girl Scout activities cost money. Camping, visits to museums and state capitals, even doing good works closer to home — they all had costs and those costs mounted up. The Girl Scouts wanted to continue their adventures and good works, so they looked around and thought,

"Hmmmm. What can we make that people will buy — lots of?"

One great idea came right out of an article on fundraising which appeared in a 1922 issue of their magazine, *The Ameri-*

can Girl. It included a recipe for delicious sugar cookies and estimates of how much money a Girl Scout Troop could make . . . by selling cookies! Girls all over the country suddenly turned to each other and said,

"That's it!! WE'LL HAVE A BAKE SALE!!!"

Groups of girls flocked to their mothers' kitchens and began to bake with a vengeance.

They mixed up the dough.
They kneaded it.
They rolled it out.
They cut it into shapes.
They used a Girl Scout trefoil-shaped cookie cutter
which cost 15 cents!
They baked the cookies.
THEN, they put those cookies in paper bags,
Stuck shiny stickers on them,
AND THEN, they marched door-to-door and sold
those cookies!

Wow, did people eat up those cookies! These cookies were a *great* idea!

Then in 1932, some smart Girl Scouts in Philadelphia thought,

"Hmmmm. How can we *increase* our sales so we have more money for hiking, and camping, and really great trips, and also help us continue to do good works?"

They came up with a *brilliant* idea. . . .

One day, some Girl Scouts paid a visit to the offices of the Philadelphia Gas Company and the Philadelphia Electric Company. They asked to see the managers and then they made their request,

"Please, could we bake our *delicious* Girl Scout cookies in your brand new electric ovens to show everyone what great cookie bakers we are?"

The managers looked at those Girl Scouts and they agreed. The Girl Scouts started baking cookies and the delicious aromas proved very effective. Everyone who *smelled* those baking cookies wanted to *buy* those cookies!

Sales were so strong that the Philadelphia Girl Scouts faced a *new* problem.

They couldn't bake enough cookies to meet the demand!

So, they came up with another *brilliant* solution. They went to visit a baking company where they asked,

"Please, will you bake our delicious vanilla cookies, using our trefoil-shaped cookie cutter, of course?

Then, please, put them in a box, so we can sell lots and lots of cookies to people?"

The baking company agreed, and in 1934 the Philadelphia Girl Scouts sold boxes filled with 44 trefoil-shaped vanilla cookies. Each box cost 23 cents. Really hungry people could buy 6 boxes for $1.35.

> *That same year, it cost 3 cents to mail a letter . . . so, do some quick arithmetic: How much does a stamp cost today? How much does a box of Girl Scout cookies cost today? Compare these costs with those of 1934!*

The *brilliant* ideas of those Philadelphia Girl Scouts caught the eye of other Girl Scouts. They stopped baking cookies at home and turned to baking companies which put delicious cookies in boxes, just like the Philadelphia Girl Scouts did. By 1936 — just two short years — Girl Scout cookie sales went national. The whole nation fell in love with Girl Scout cookies.

Girl Scout cookies thrive to this day. They come in many varieties, and their bright, colorful boxes have photographs which show girls at their best — smiling wide, and proving to all who eat them, that these girls are some of the smartest cookies in America!

Girl Scout Cookies

EARLY COOKIE SALES by Girl Scouts occurred in Oklahoma, New York, Connecticut and Pennsylvania shortly after Juliette Low founded the Girl Scouts in 1912. The Philadelphia Council of Girl Scouts is recognized by the Girl Scouts of the USA as the originator of the modern Girl Scout cookie and cookie sale. About 2 million Girl Scouts sell Girl Scout cookies each year to earn money for program activities, special events and projects, and for purchasing and maintaining equipment and facilities. A sign placed by the Pennsylvania State and Historical Commission at 1401 Arch Street in Philadelphia marks the site of the 1932 bake sale.

Girl Scouts® is a registered trademark of Girl Scouts of the USA.

Boy Scout Jamborees!

THERE WAS A TIME many years ago when hundreds, no *thousands* of people camped on the hills of Valley Forge. They came to Valley Forge from so many different states. They practiced their marksmanship, they did patrols, and at night, they gathered around big campfires and sang songs.

And they ate. My goodness, did they eat!

On any given day, they ate beef that came from 1330 heads of steer.

They drank 74,480 quarts of milk.

And they chowed down on chicken legs that came from 26,600 chickens.

Most of all they ate hot dogs. *Lots* of hot dogs. In fact, if you lined up all those hot dogs, they would have stretched for 17 *miles!*

Now wait a minute. *Hot dogs?* This doesn't quite fit the image most people have of Valley Forge. That's the place where George Washington and his army camped during the Revolutionary War. *Everyone* knows they had a hard winter and there wasn't a lot of food.

More to the point, there weren't lots of hot dogs because there was no such *thing* as a hot dog back in 1777–78, though the soldiers might have enjoyed a sausage or two on a very lucky day.

No, the people who drank all that milk and ate all those hot dogs were not the men in tattered uniforms who shivered in Valley Forge back in 1777–78.

These people wore clean and crisp khaki and olive uniforms, with neckerchiefs of all different colors. And, they had badges — lots of badges . . .

Because, they were Boy Scouts! *Lots* of Boy Scouts — about 50,000 of them to be exact. Back in 1950, 1957 and again in 1964, Boy Scouts, Explorers and adult leaders came to Valley Forge for the National Boy Scout Jamboree. For four days, all those Boy Scouts built brotherhood and friendship — and what better place to do that than Valley Forge, the place where George Washington and his army spent that legendary winter.

They came from every state in the union — including Hawaii and Alaska. There were even Boy Scouts from other countries. Some came in cars and buses, but 25,000 of the 50,000 traveled by train, courtesy of the nation's rail systems which offered special rates and special menus in their dining cars. If the menu was anything like the one at Valley Forge, it included the Boy Scout special — hot dogs.

Once at Valley Forge, the Boy Scouts spread out over 1500 acres of land. There were 38 different camp sites and each had 34 Boy Scout troops.

So, did these Boy Scouts rough it, just like those soldiers who were at Valley Forge with George Washington?

They did live in tents, not in the warm and dry huts which Washington's men built and used. So, maybe that was a bit rougher.

But the Boy Scouts also had food and luxuries that Washington's men could not have even imagined.

For starters, they had water. The Jamboree set up its own sewer system, piping in 1.5 million gallons of water a day to meet the various needs of those 50,000 males. This meant that each person used 30 gallons of water — per day!

Each of the 38 camp sites had its own health lodge with three doctors and four aides ready to hand out bandages, or more than bandages if needed.

There was electricity! And a newspaper, *The Jamboree Journal!* There were telephone lines and a telephone number, Jamboree 3–7100! There was a press tent ready to handle newspaper, radio, and television coverage throughout the na-

tion. And there were clergy who conducted religious services of all types.

Over the course of their four days, the Boy Scouts shared memorable experiences. They raised the flag every morning. They demonstrated various camping skills. They learned about forestry and conservation. They held songfests. And on the last day, they held a massive pageant which celebrated the Jamboree's theme — "Onward for God and My Country." All in this same place where George Washington and his army camped so many years before.

When the pageant was over, those 50,000 Boy Scouts returned to their homes. The city of tents disappeared, along with the sewer lines and the phone number and the *The Jamboree Journal.* All gone — except for the memories held dear by the thousands of men and boys who once came.

Maybe some of those memories include . . . hot dogs??

Boy Scouts at Valley Forge

BOY SCOUTS HAVE CAMPED at Valley Forge since 1913, honoring the legacy of General George Washington and the valiant Continental Army who camped on these same hills during the winter of 1777–78. In addition to these annual events which draw mostly Scouts from the immediate area, there were three national Boy Scout Jamborees which drew thousands from all over the country. At the first of these in 1950, President Harry S. Truman and General Dwight Eisenhower addressed the participants. Vice President Richard Nixon addressed the Jamboree of 1957. The last national Jamboree occurred in 1964. Local Boy Scouts still camp and have events in Valley Forge keeping that tradition alive.

How to Become a Storyteller

PEOPLE LOVE STORIES. Grandparents like to tell stories about when they were kids to their grandkids. Friends like to tell stories about something amazing or funny or awful to their pals while riding the bus. TV shows tell stories. So do movies and plays. People read stories in books. Sometimes they read them aloud so others can hear. Sometimes they read silently just for their own pleasure. No matter what our age or interest, nearly everybody loves a great story.

What Makes a Story Great?

Stories come in all different shapes and sizes and forms. But a great story generally has . . .

★ A good **beginning,** an interesting **middle,** and a tie-it-all up **end.**

★ A **main character or characters,** whether human, animal, vegetable, mineral or . . . (use your imagination!) This main character is the "star" of the story.

★ A **central event,** around which the story revolves. The event can be funny, it can be dramatic, it can be life-changing, it can be odd, it can be amazing.

A great story also . . .

★ **Engages our senses and imagination.** It encourages us to "see" or "smell" or "feel" even if we are just listening or reading.

★ **Engages our emotions.** A story can make us sad or happy or even laugh out loud.

★ **Often makes us think and ask questions.** What would I have done in that situation? What would it be like to live back then? How is my life similar or different?

★ **Can pass down history** or important information. For thousands of years people didn't write their history, they *told* their history from one generation to the next.

★ Or, **might have a moral.** Does this story offer an important lesson?

Think about a story *you* like. What makes this story special to you? What is it about? Why do you enjoy it? Why do you want to read it more than once, or hear it over and over, or tell it to your friends? If *you* like this story, chances are someone else will like it too, and that can be a great story to start with if you want to be a storyteller.

What Makes a Great Storyteller?

A Storyteller shares a story with another person. A Storyteller works hard to tell a good story and also give a good performance. A Storyteller brings a story to life by using her voice and body to help give meaning and add interest. For example, if a story includes . . .

★ something about a hammer, a Storyteller might use his hand and pretend to hold a hammer, and then pretend to use it to hammer a nail.

★ a scary part, the Storyteller can use a scary voice and scary gestures to make the story even . . . scarier!

★ a conversation between two people, the Storyteller will play both roles, for example, using a high voice for a woman and a low voice for a man.

★ an animal, the Storyteller might "become" that animal, making sounds like a horse, or a cat, or a chicken.

All of this makes for a great story presented by a great Storyteller. It takes some work and practice, but can be a lot of fun.

Getting Ready

Pick a story you like. If it is *written*, like the stories in this book, read it several times. Ask some questions:

★ How does the story start?
★ What happens?
★ How does it end?
★ What is the plot of the story?
★ Who is the star of the story?
★ Who are the other characters in the story?
★ When does it take place and where?
★ If there is written dialogue, what do the characters say and how do you imagine them saying it?

If it is an oral story, a story that someone has told you but is not written down, make some notes while asking these questions:

★ What is the main event of the story?
★ How does the story start? What happens? How does it end?
★ Who is the "star"?
★ Who are the other characters?
★ Where does it take place?
★ What sticks out as the most memorable part of the story — the funniest part, the most dramatic part, the saddest part?

Now, close your eyes and use your imagination. Think about the "world" of your story:

★ What does the place look like where the story happens?
★ What do the people look like? Are they young? Old? Male? Female?
★ What clothes are they wearing?
★ What do their voices sound like?
★ Are there special noises in your story? Or smells? Or tastes? Or actions?
★ How does the story make you *feel?* Happy, sad, amused, thoughtful, amazed?

Open your eyes and think about your story. Make notes about important facts or ideas or plot details. It often helps to write out the story for yourself using your own words. If you do, remember to have a good beginning, middle, and end, and an interesting central character — the "star." Use your imagination to bring the story to life.

Create the Story and Practice Storytelling

★ Find a private place where no one can see or hear you.

★ Pretend someone is in the room with you.

★ Tell your story! Practice it, get the details right.

★ Make your characters lively and interesting.

★ Find a great punch line to end the story.

One trick to get started is to read the written version of your story aloud. Do it with drama and flair. Then, when you feel ready, put the written version aside and tell the story without it. Storytellers don't read aloud from books. Practice the story so that you know it well and feel ready to share it with a friend.

Perform the Story!

It's time to take the stage. Close your book. Hide your notes. Find a friend. Tell your story!

When you have finished, ask your friend if she liked the story. Ask her:

★ Was my story interesting?

★ What did you like?

★ Was there anything you didn't understand?

★ What would make the story better and more fun to listen to?

Then, look at the original story.

★ Did you forget anything important?

★ What changes would make the story better?

★ What changes would make the presentation — the Storytelling — better?

Now, find *another* friend. Tell your story again, adding your improvements. Ask him for his comments, and think some more about what you can do to tell the story even better the next time. Then do it again! Just keep practicing until you know that both the story and your performance are "just right." You will know when they are right because it will feel easy and natural for you to tell the story. Listeners will pay close attention. And they will laugh. Or cry. But best of all, they will applaud! That's when you know you are a Storyteller!

Remember: Practice makes perfect and the best storytellers spend a lot of time making sure that they have put together a great story AND a great performance.

Story Topics

Early Pennsylvania History

Lachimo, Lenape Storyteller

Broomsticks in Pennsylvania

Revolutionary War

Lydia Darragh, Quaker Spy

General Howe and the Cow

Battle of the Kegs

Rebecca Franks: Tory Teen and Party Queen

Allen McLane: Master Spy

The Day Charles Willson Peale Almost Blew Up
Philadelphia

The Vexillologist

Women's History

Lydia Darragh, Quaker Spy

General Howe and the Cow

Rebecca Franks: Tory Teen and Party Queen

Escape from the President's House: The Amazing Story
of Oney Judge

Doctor Mom

Cross That Line! Harriet Tubman and the Underground
Railroad

The Vexillologist

Smart Cookies!

African-American/Underground Railroad/Civil War

The Sailor and Isaac Hopper: Inventors of the
Underground Railroad?

Escape from the President's House: The Amazing Story
of Oney Judge

Cross That Line! Harriet Tubman and the Underground
Railroad

It Be Me, Peter

Thirty-Four Stars: Abraham Lincoln Visits
Independence Hall

Inventors

Battle of the Kegs

The Day Charles Willson Peale Almost Blew Up
Philadelphia

The Sailor and Isaac Hopper: Inventors of the
Underground Railroad?

Up, Up and Away

The Birth of Television

Smart Cookies!

Just For Fun!

The Day Charles Willson Peale Almost Blew Up
Philadelphia

Pirates!

Smart Cookies!

Boy Scout Jamborees

Bibliography

THE SOURCES CITED below include those archival collections, books, journal articles, and websites which grounded the factual content and background for each story in this book. Some of these sources are original manuscripts and rare books which are less available. Most of the books, however, are in print. *Philadelphia: A 300 Year History* (New York: W.W. Norton, 1983) offers an excellent overall history of the city from 1682 through the 1980s. It has a detailed index. The richness of materials available on websites opens a wealth of resources that offer paths to learn more. That said, it is important to use websites that are reliable and whose information can be substantiated in other sources. Every effort was made to assure that the websites used for these stories fulfills those requirements.

Lachimo, Lenape Storyteller

Edwin Wolf, *Philadelphia, Portrait of an American City.* Harrisburg, PA: Stackpole Books, 1975, p. 20.

Frank G. Speck, *A Study of the Delaware Indians Big House Ceremony.* Harrisburg, PA: Publications of the Pennsylvania Historical Commission, vol. 2, 1931.

http://www.delawaretribeofindians.usn.us/village.html

http://www.geocities.com/shabak_waxtju/story.html

http://henryhahn.net/myths/lenapecreation.html

http://www.phillywater.org/Delaware/Watershed/history_
watershed.htm

http://www.statemuseumpa.org/Potamkin/brother/part2.
htm

Broomsticks in Pennsylvania

John Fanning Watson, *Annals of Philadelphia, Volume I.*
Philadelphia: Edwin S. Stuart, 1884, pp. 265–6, 274–5.

Russell Weigley, ed., *Philadelphia: A 300 Year History.* New
York: W.W. Norton, 1983, pp.1–32.

Lydia Darragh, Quaker Spy

"Lydia Darragh," *Notable American Women: A Biographical Dictionary.* Cambridge, MA: Belknap Press, 1971, pp.
434–5.

John Fanning Watson, *Annals of Philadelphia and Pennsylvania, Volume II.* Philadelphia: Edwin S. Stuart, 1884,
pp. 327 and 385.

"Lydia Darragh," http://www.americanrevolution.org/women
15.html

"LydiaBarringtonDarragh,"http://www.nmwh.org/Education
/biography_ldarragh.html

Elizabeth Leonard, *All the Daring of the Soldier: Women of the
Civil War Armies.* New York: Norton, 1999, see chapter 1
for story of Lydia Darragh.

"Lydia Darragh," http://www.ushistory.org/march/bio/lydia.
htm

Thomas J. McGuire, *The Philadelphia Campaign: Germantown and the Roads to Valley Forge, Volume II*. Mechanicsburg, PA: Stackpole Books, 2007, p. 240.

General Howe and the Cow

Thomas J. McGuire, *The Philadelphia Campaign: Brandywine and the Fall of Philadelphia, Volume I*. Mechanicsburg, PA, 2006, p. 280. The story of Jane and General Howe is one of a series of stories about the Gibbons family recounted by McGuire in his book.

Note: Nearly all the conversation between Jane Gibbons and General Howe which appears is this story is as it was recorded.

Wayne Bodle, *Valley Forge Winter: Civilians and Soldiers in War*. University Park, PA: Penn State Press, 2002, see Chapter 8, "The Lord's Time to Work," pp. 163–184.

The Battle of the Kegs

Thomas J. McGuire, *The Philadelphia Campaign: Germantown and the Roads to Valley Forge*. Mechanicsburg, PA: Stackpole Books, 2007.

Russell Weigley, ed., *Philadelphia: A 300 Year History*. New York: W.W. Norton, 1983, p. 137.

"Battle of the Kegs," http://www.americanrevolution.org/warsongs55.html

"The Turtle and the Battle of the Kegs," http://www.doublegv.com/ggv/battles/TheTurtle.html

Rebecca Franks: Tory Teen and Party Queen

Morris Bishop, "You Are Invited to a Mischianza," *American Heritage Magazine,* August 1974, Volume 25, Issue 5, from: http://americanheritage.com/articles/magazine/ah/1974/5/1974_5_69.shtml

Benson Lossing, *Pictorial Field Book of the Revolution, Volume II,* 1850, "Major Andre's Description of the Mischianza." From http://freepages.history.rootsweb.com/~wcarr1/Lossing1Chap36a.html

"Rebecca Franks,"*Notable American Women: A Biographical Dictionary,* Volume I. Cambridge, MA: Harvard University Press, 1971, pp. 664–5.

"Rebecca Franks," http://www.americanrevolution.org/women16html

Russell Weigley, ed, *Philadelphia: A 300–Year History.* NY: W.W. Norton, 1982, pp. 140–43.

Allen McLane, Master Spy

Wayne Bodle, *Valley Forge Winter: Civilians and Soldiers in War.* University Park, PA: Penn State Press, 2002, pp. 235–6.

Fred J. Cook, "Allen McLane: Unknown Hero of the Revolution," *American Heritage Magazine,* October 1956, Issue 6.

Thomas Fleming, *Washington's Secret War: The Hidden History of Valley Forge.* New York: Harper Collins, 2006.

John Fanning Watson, *Annals of Philadelphia and Pennsylvania, Volume II.* Philadelphia: Edwin Stuart, 1884, pp. 321–24.

"Who Served Here" Allan McLane: Continental Officer, http://www.ushistory.org/valleyforge/served/mclane.html

"The First Generation of United States Marshals, Allan McLane, The First Marshall of Delaware" http://www.usmarshals.gov/history/firstmarshals/mclane.htm

Encounter between Capt. Allan McLane and a British dragoon at Frankfort, near Philadelphia. Painting by James Peale. 111–SC-91311. (revolutionary_war_039.jpg)

The Day Charles Willson Peale Almost Blew Up Philadelphia

Gary Nash, *First City: Philadelphia and the Forging of Historical Memory*. Philadelphia: University of Pennsylvania Press, 2001, pp. 134–5.

See also:

David McCullough, *1776*. New York: Simon and Schuster, 2005.

Russell Weigley, *Philadelphia: A 300 Year History*. New York: W.W. Norton, 1983, pp. 155–257, "The Federal City, 1783–1800," and "The Athens of America, 1800–1825."

Lillian B. Miller, ed, *The Peale Family: Creation of a Legacy, 1770–1870*. Abbeville Press, in association with the Trust for Museum Exhibitions and the National Portrait Gallery, Smithsonian Institution, c. 1996. See especially, David C. Ward, "Democratic Culture: The Peale Museums, 1784–1850," pp. 260–275.

http://www.ansp.org/museum/jefferson/otherPages/peale_
museum.php—website of the Academy of Natural Sciences, Philadelphia

Irwin Richman, "Charles Willson Peale and the Philadelphia
Museum," *Pennsylvania History*, July 1962, pp. 257–277.

Escape From the President's House:
The Amazing Story of Oney Judge

Edward Lawlor, Jr, "Oney Judge," http://www.ushistory
.org/presidentshouse/slaves/oney/htm

"Ona Maria Judge," http://www.weekslibrary.org/ona_
maria_judge.htm

"Washington's Runaway Slave," from *The Granite Freeman*,
New Hampshire, May 22, 1845, reprinted in Frank W.
Miller's *Portsmouth New Hampshire Weekly*, June 2, 1877,
under the title "Washington's Runaway Slave, and How
Portsmouth Freed Her," Author: Rev. T.H. Adams; and,
"1846 Interview with Ona Judge Staines," by the Rev. Ben-
jamin Chase, Letter to the Editor, The Liberator, January
1, 1847. As quoted in *Slave Testimony, Two Centuries of
Letters, Speeches, Interviews, and Autobiographies*, John W.
Blasingame, ed., Baton Rouge and London: Louisiana
State University Press, 1977, pp. 248–50.

Cited in http://www.ushistory.org/presidentshouse/slaves/
oneyinterview.htm

Up, Up and Away

Pamela Lowry, "Benjamin Franklin and Friends lay the Basis for Manned Flight," from *The New Federalist*, January 16, 2006, Volume XX, No. 2, http://www.schillerinstitute.org/educ/hist/Franklin_flight.html

Christine Sternberg Patrick, "Washington Supports 'bold AERONAUT," from *The Papers of George Washington News*, Number 4, Summer 2001. www.virginia.edu/gwpapers

"Jean-Pierre Blanchard," http://www.centennialofflight.gov/essay/Dictionary/blanchard/D110.htm

"This Month in Physics History, November 1783: Intrepid Physicist is First to Fly," http://www.aps.org/publications/aspnews/200611/history.cfm

Pirates!

ACE Group Archival Materials for the Insurance Company of North America, manuscripts about the *Pigou* and William Sansom.

The Sailor and Isaac Hopper: Inventors of the Underground Railroad?

Fergus Bordewich, *Bound for Canaan: The Epic Story of the Underground Railroad, America's First Civil Rights Movement.* New York: Amistad, 2005, pp. 46–63.

"Isaac Hopper," http:www.bchistory.org/beavercounty.booklengthdocuments/AMilobook/16Hopper.html

Anna L. Curtis, *Stories of the Underground Railroad*, "Lawyer to the Negro: Isaac T. Hopper," Island Workshop Press, Co-oop, Inc., 1941. Reproduced in http://www.shockfamily .net/underground/isaachopper.html
www.pbs.org/wgbh/aia/part3/3p249.html

Doctor Mom
Sandra Mackenzie Lloyd, "Eighteenth Century Medicine," *1787: The Day-To-Day Story of the Constitutional Convention*, compiled by the Historians of Independence National Historical Park. New York: Exeter Books, 1987, pp. 45–6.
The Wyck Papers, Hannah Haines Collection, on deposit at the American Philosophical Society of Pennsylvania.

Cross That Line! Harriet Tubman and the Underground Railroad
Fergus Bordewich, *Bound for Canaan: The Epic Story of the Underground Railroad, America's First Civil Rights Movement*. New York: Amistad Press, 2005, pp. 344–355.
John Hope Franklin, "Harriet Tubman," *Notable American Women: A Biographical Dictionary*. Cambridge, MA: Belknap Press of Harvard University Press, 1971, pp. 481–483.
Kate Clifford Larson, *Racing for Freedom: Harriet Tubman's Underground Railroad Network in Maryland and Delaware*, http://www.harriettubmanjournal.com/

It Be Me, Peter

Fergus M. Bordewich, *Bound for Canaan: The Epic Story of the Underground Railroad, America's First Civil Rights Movement.* New York: Amistad, 2005, pp. 356–57.

George and Willene Hendrick, eds., *Fleeing for Freedom: Stories of the Underground Railroad as Told by Levi Coffin and William Still.* Chicago: Ivan R. Dee, 2004.

James Oliver Horton, "Flight to Freedom: One Family and the Story of the Underground Railroad," Organization of American Historians, http://www.oah.org/pubs/magazine/family/horton.html

James Oliver Horton, "William Still: From Slave Catcher to Conductor," http://www.slaveryinamerica.org/narratives/bio_william_still.htm

William Still, *The Underground Railroad: Authentic Narratives and First-Hand Accounts.* Mineola, NY: Dover Publications, 2007.

Linn Washington, "The Chronicle of an American First Family," http://www.undergroundrr.com/firstfamily.html

Thirty-Four Stars: Abraham Lincoln Visits Independence Hall

Archives of Independence National Historical Park, Philadelphia *Evening Bulletin,* February 12, 1918. This includes the story about Charles W. Alexander and his recollections of the day Abraham Lincoln visited Independence Hall.

Charlene Mires, *Independence Hall in American Memory.*

Philadelphia: University of Pennsylvania Press, 2002, pp. 107–110.

J. Rickard, "Siege of Fort Sumter, 12–13 April 1861," November 3, 2006, http://www.historyofwar.org/articles/battles_sumter_html

Russell Weigley, ed., *Philadelphia: A 300 Year History*. New York: Norton, 1982, 393–4. http://www.si.edu/Encyclopedia_si/nmah/flag.htm

The Vexillologist

"Betsy Ross," *Notable American Women: A Biographical Dictionary*. Cambridge, MA: Belknap Press of Harvard University, 1971, pp. 198–99.

"Charles H. Weisgerber and The Betsy Ross Memorial Association," http://www.sas.upenn.edu/~ctd/Walter/chw.htm

Laurel Thatcher Ulrich, "How Betsy Ross Got Famous," *Common-Place*. October 2007, http://www.common-place.org/vol-08/no-01/ulrich

www.ushistory.org/betsy/more/weisgerber.htm

www.betsyrosshouse.org/hist_house/

www.betsyrosshouse.org/hist_woman/

The Birth of Television: The Philo T. Farnsworth Story

Hal Landen, "The Birth of Television," from Paul Schatzkin, "Farnsworth Chronicles," http://www.farnovision.com/

Neil Postman, "Philo Farnsworth," *Time*, March 29, 1999.

Paul Schatzkin, *The Boy Who Invented Television: A Story of Inspiration, Persistence and Quiet Passion.* TeamCom Books, 2002.

Smart Cookies

There are some discrepancies of date about when the Philadelphia Girl Scouts first sold cookies at the Philadelphia Electric and Gas Companies. The correct information is found in:

" 'C' is For Cookie," in *A Celebration of 75 Years of Girl Scouting in Greater Philadelphia,* 1992.

Additional background about the Girl Scouts and cookie sales may be found in:

"Girl Scout Cookie History" http://www.girlscouts.org/program/gs_cookies/cookie_history/

Pennsylvania Historical and Museum Commission, State Marker program, http://www.phmc.state.pa.us/bah/DOH/descriptresults.asp?markertext=scouts&secid=31

"Our Girl Scout Cookie Sale"

http://cheesecakeandfriends.com/troop1440/1999/cookies.htm

"Girl Scout Cookie Fact Sheet"

http://www.girlscoutsmcc.org/pdfs/cookie%20sale%2006/06%20Cookie%20Fact%20Sheet.pdf

"FAQs - GirlScoutCookiesABC"

http://www.girlscoutcookiesabc.com/sa/faqs.asp

"Bites of Cookie History"

http://www.gsmpc.org/cook_bites.pdf
"Girl Scout Cookies"
http://everything2.com/index.pl?node=girl%20scout%20
    cookies
"Girl Scouts: Definition and Much More"
http://www.answers.com/topic/scouting

Boy Scout Jamborees!
Valley Forge National Historical Park Archives, Boy Scout
    Jamborees: press materials, newspaper articles
http://ww.ushistory.org/valleyforge/youasked/025.htm
www.worldofscoutingmuseum.org

Contributors

Stories

Ralph Archbold Team: Marie-Claire Archbold, Ralph Archbold, J. Nathan Bazzel, Patricia Stallone, K. Ward Vinson

Lydia Darragh, Quaker Spy

Up, Up and Away

It Be Me, Peter

Thirty-Four Stars: Abraham Lincoln Visits Independence Hall

Andi Coyle

Pirates!

Mitchell Kramer

Lachimo, Lenape Storyteller

Sandra Mackenzie Lloyd

General Howe and the Cow

Rebecca Franks: Tory Teen and Party Queen

Allen McLane: Master Spy

The Day Charles Willson Peale Almost Blew Up Philadelphia

Escape from the President's House: The Amazing Story of Oney Judge

The Sailor and Isaac Hopper: Inventors of the Underground
     Railroad?
Doctor Mom
Cross That Line! Harriet Tubman and the Underground
     Railroad
The Birth of Television
Boy Scout Jamboree!
Rebecca Odorisio
     Smart Cookies
Steve Seyfried
     The Vexillologist
Ed Stivender
     Broomsticks in Pennsylvania
     The Battle of the Kegs

Illustrations

Katrina Damkoehler

Historic Philadelphia, Inc.
and *Once Upon A Nation*

HISTORIC PHILADELPHIA, INC. is a non-profit organization founded in 1994 by then-Mayor Edward G. Rendell. Historic Philadelphia, Inc. brings history to life for visitors with first person interpreters who portray Colonial Americans ranging from Benjamin Franklin and Betsy Ross, to everyday workers and trades people. It also maintains the historic Betsy Ross House and the newly renovated Franklin Square where visitors can enjoy beautiful green space, ride the *Philadelphia Park Liberty Carousel*, or play miniature golf on a course with a distinctive Philadelphia flavor.

Historic Philadelphia, Inc.'s *Once Upon A Nation* program launched in Philadelphia in 2005 and in Valley Forge National Historical Park in 2007. *Once Upon A Nation* offers engaging tours which immerse visitors in the places, stories and people central to our country's founding. *Once Upon A Nation* also offers its signature Storytelling program in both locations seven days a week from Memorial Day to Labor Day. In this free program, Storytellers welcome visitors to inviting benches, tell their amazing and true stories, and then give each person a star to add to their Storytelling flag. Please come visit!

For more information see www.historicphiladelphia.org

Historic Philadelphia, Inc. makes our nation's history relevant and real through interpretation, interaction and education, strengthening Greater Philadelphia's role as the destination to experience American history.

Thanks to Our Friends

Special Friends of this Book
Geoffrey Berwind
Holly Carlson
V. Chapman-Smith
Wendy Dyer-Ayres
Daria Fink
Catherine Almy Hineline
Eileen Honert
Joan Lowe
Amy Malissa
Tom McGuire
Sue Michel
Eli & Seth Needle
Anna Coxe Toogood

Partner Organizations and their Wonderful Staffs
Arch Street Meeting
Betsy Ross House
Carpenters' Company of the City and County of Philadelphia
City Tavern
Christ Church
Elfreth's Alley
Greater Philadelphia Tourism Marketing Corporation
Independence National Historical Park
Independence Visitor Center Corporation
International Storytelling Center
National Constitution Center
National Museum of American Jewish History
Valley Forge National Historical Park

Funding Partners
ACE-INA Foundation
American Revolution Patriots' Fund
Avery Foundation
City of Philadelphia
Commonwealth of Pennsylvania
Lenfest Foundation
Lincoln Financial Foundation
Pennsylvania Humanities Council
PNC
Religious Society of Free Quakers
Valley Forge Convention and Visitor's Bureau

Special Friends of Once Upon A Nation Storytelling
Ralph Appelbaum
Ralph Archbold
Mary Bomar
Frances Delmar
Meryl Levitz
William Moore
Dennis Reidenbach
The Honorable Edward G. Rendell
Wayne Spilove and the Board of Directors, Historic
    Philadelphia, Inc.
The Staff, Actors and Storytellers of Historic
    Philadelphia, Inc.